WHAT IN
HEAVEN
IS GOING ON AT
CHURCH?

WHAT IN
HEAVEN
IS GOING ON AT
CHURCH?

I Visited 100+ Churches to Find Out!

BUDDY GRIFFIN

TATE PUBLISHING
AND ENTERPRISES, LLC

Published by Tate Publishing & Enterprises, LLC
127 E. Trade Center Terrace | Mustang, Oklahoma 73064 USA
1.888.361.9473 | www.tatepublishing.com

Tate Publishing is committed to excellence in the publishing industry. The company reflects the philosophy established by the founders, based on Psalm 68:11,
"The Lord gave the word and great was the company of those who published it."

Book design copyright © 2016 by Tate Publishing, LLC. All rights reserved.
Cover design by Joana Quilantang
Interior design by Jomar Ouano

Published in the United States of America

ISBN: 978-1-68254-943-8
1. Religion / Christian Ministry / Pastoral Resources
2. Religion / Christian Church / General
16.01.19

Acknowledgments

The following people had some part in writing this book. They prayed with me, for me, and assisted me in many ways. They shared godly advice, influencing opinions, constructive suggestions, and lots of encouragement, which helped produce the book you are holding. I love and appreciate all of them, and they can't do a thing about it!

A very special *thank you* and *I love you* goes to the love of my life, my wife, Sandy.

- Dr. Denny Autrey
- Dr. Tom Billings
- James Birdsong
- Dr. John Bisagno
- James Bouvier
- Dwain Camp
- Daniel Davis
- Tim Donham
- Dr. Josh Ellis
- Dr. Frank Estes
- Tammy Fort
- Richard Headrick
- Dr. Don Keathly
- Bryan Lambert
- Jim and Pam Laucher
- Dr. Robert Lewis
- Wayne Martin
- Dr. Gregg Matte
- Carl Miller
- Dr. John Morgan
- Buck Oliphant
- Judge Paul Pressler
- Scott Reichling
- Dr. Skip Smith
- Jerry Squyres
- Patrick Stewart
- Wick Stuckey
- Kit Sublett
- Roger Wernette
- Rick Wertz
- Cecil Whitton
- Gary Williams

A big word of thanks and appreciation goes to all the staff at Tate Publishing.

CONTENTS

Upon retirement, I became *a secret church shopper* to discover how other churches "do church." Along the journey, I learned some heavy life lessons and fell in love with God all over again. I want to share with pastors and churches information to help advance God's kingdom.

When a visitor drives into a church parking lot, their visiting experience begins. Signage, how they are greeted, and the appearance of the facilities all play a part in their perception of the church. Let's check it out. Go to church with me and let's see what in heaven is going on.

There is a problem when a church spends four minutes in a Sunday morning worship service making announcements and promoting events and twenty-two seconds in prayer. Why isn't there more prayer, individually and collectively, in our churches? A church leads on its knees—it is the strongest position a church can take.

The *CPR* I am referring to is spiritual life giving—*Christ-produced revival.* There is not a program or ministry that can bring life to a church unless Jesus is in charge. This is the greatest need of the church today!

Based on the fable of the "Frog in the Pot," is it possible that a church could gradually allow things that are unbiblical to come into their family and not be aware of it? Could they have traditions they have practiced for so long that the warm waters of complacency have numbed them to the true gospel message?

After 16 months of visiting 115 churches and 28 denominations, I am not the same person I was when I began. God has educated me in remarkable ways. Please hear my heart.

Real life is often funnier than comedy. You can't attend 115 churches and not have some crazy things happen. Read on and let's laugh together.

Final thoughts and conclusions to wind up my incredible journey. For the glory of God, may it all make a difference for His kingdom!

PREFACE

What in Heaven Is Going On at Church? is the name of a church-visiting project that turned out to be a book. My sixteen-month journey has been eye-opening, awe-inspiring, and spiritually maturing—an adventure that has caused me to fall in love with Christ and His church all over again.

The word *church* is used over nine hundred times in this book. By definition, the word *church* refers to all genuine believers in Jesus Christ—all those who have placed their faith in Him for salvation and have been born again. They come from various denominations and live in many locations around the world. This group of believers is sometimes referred to as the body of Christ, the family of God, the bride of Christ, the invisible church, or the universal church.

A specific segment of the overall body of Christ that meets together regularly at a specific location is also referred to as a *church*. And many times, we use the word *church* in speaking of the actual building where a local congregation meets. All three of these meanings of the word *church* will be used in this book.

About midway through my visits to churches, I walked into what was obviously a recently constructed church building. I was immediately impressed by the attractive decor, and I could smell that pleasant, "new" facility scent. The building seemed functional and well planned. Excitement filled the air as the friendliness of the church members welcomed me inside. I immediately noticed near the entrance a large art installation on a wall, highlighted by a soft spotlight. The piece was well displayed and definitely caught the attention of everyone upon entering. It read:

I AM YOUR CHURCH

I am your church. I am here because you
built me. I am beautifully situated in your midst.
In the center of your neighborhood I will be a
cherished landmark to the people who will come
to my door in the coming years. You built me,
remember, because you know your life is incomplete
without me.
I am your church. But I am not here simply to adorn.
I am here to serve. Your children and your growing youth
come to me to be taught the ways of the Lord. Your
brides and grooms come to my altar so their marriages
will be sanctified by divine blessings.
I am your church. I comfort your sick and sorrowing.
I bury your dead and offer rest to the weary. Pardon
and peace are my message to the sin-burdened soul.
My message of mercy brings new life. To your aged
I give courage and security. I cause their children to
call me blessed.
I am your church. My doors are open to all—rich or
poor, bound or free. My pulpit rings out the message
of good will to men, of peace and pardon, and a Savior's
love to all. I teach you the way of life and guide you on
the road to heaven.
I am your church. Come and worship. Support me,
and I will serve you all your days.

As spoken by
Bishop Franklin G. Jones
February 7, 1982

After thoughtfully reading through the piece a second time, I took a picture with my iPhone. There is much to ponder in those four short paragraphs. I paused and really began to think. Thoughts about the church, Christ's bride, began to fill my mind. Love and praise for Jesus Christ overflowed from my heart. Later on, my own personal thoughts continued:

- I know Jesus established the church to carry out His work on earth.
- I believe in the church. I love the church.
- I support the mission of the church.
- I value the importance and impact of the church.
- I pray for the church, its pastors, its staff people, and members.
- I would never intentionally do anything to tear down or hurt the church in any way—I want only to make it healthier and stronger.
- I see the main purpose of the church as being to worship, praise, and honor God while proclaiming the eternal, life-changing message of salvation through Jesus Christ!
- I am confident that no matter what happens, the church will survive! What has happened in the past, what is going on now, and what challenges come in the future—the church cannot be destroyed!
- I consider it to be an exciting and humbling privilege to be a part of Christ's church, the family of God.

The quote by Bishop Jones speaks of the physical building and the ministries of the real church, the body of Christ, that the building represents. The real church takes Jesus out of the church building into a dark world every day. The real church is made up of all born-again Christ followers who are all called by God and equipped to serve.

The actual physical building is a gathering place, a hospital for sinners, a safe haven for believers, where the family of God comes together to pray, study His Word, minister to each other, recharge spiritual batteries, seek Christ's leadership, praise His name, get fired up, and go out as soldiers of the cross, ready to charge hell with a water pistol. We proclaim the greatest message ever heard: "Jesus saves, Jesus saves!"

I have never taken lightly my commitment to gather reliable firsthand information from the 100+ churches I attended. I have prayerfully sought to share the information gleaned in kindness and love and in the most constructive manner possible to honor our Lord Jesus Christ. My mission is one of encouragement across denominational lines to every pastor, staff person, and lay leader in the entire body of Christ.

The primary purpose of my church-visiting project and the resulting book has been to provide firsthand information for the church to advance the kingdom of God. It is my prayerful hope that, through the content of this book, my purpose will be accomplished!

*Let it be for the edification of the church
that you seek to excel.*

—1 Corinthians 14:12 (NIV)

1

Why I Visited 100+ Churches

How It All Began

In the beginning, I did not have a plan in place to do what I did. It came about gradually. In fact, you might say the whole thing evolved—and I never dreamed what was going to take place!

I had made the decision to retire about a year in advance of doing so. I have always been a high-energy, constantly active, let's-get-things-done kind of guy. I loved what I was doing as I served in full-time church ministry. I had no long-range plan to retire at a certain age and no idea what I might do with my time if I did retire (except go bass fishing—a lot!). But the day came when I knew it was time.

I have always believed that when God calls you into ministry, it is a lifetime deal. It has always been my desire to serve Him faithfully for my entire life, and I would much rather "wear out" than "rust out." My idea of retirement is *re-tire-ment*—I just traded in the set of tires I had been running on for fifty years. I replaced them with a new set of tough, high-quality tires to carry me along the new road God is leading me on until I cross the finish line of life on this earth.

So during the last months of my church staff service, I began training people to carry on the ministry without my leadership, and I began praying about what God would lead me to do with my time.

Since my wife and I intended to remain as members at our current church, I realized from a practical standpoint that it would be better for me to "disappear" from my church for a while. Ministry leadership replacements deserve a chance to establish themselves without the rather awkward and even intimidating presence of the former regime. On the other hand, what was I supposed to do on Sunday mornings? Watch TV church services? Sleep in? After working for a lifetime, many retirees wake up the day after asking themselves, *Now what?*

To answer my own question, I thought this would be a great opportunity to visit some other churches to see how they "do church." Every pastor is interested in what's going on among their sister churches. They often hear reports (positive and negative), but that's about it. The more I thought about it, the more I liked it. I have always wondered what was really going on in all those churches I drove by on Sunday mornings on the way to *my* church. Now I had a chance to find out, and I was excited about it!

GETTING STARTED

On the first Sunday after my official retirement, I selected a church and set off to visit. I could not remember the last time I had attended a church service at a church other than my own, where I was strictly a visitor with no particular responsibilities or agenda. I've been in many churches through the years, where I had been invited to preach, lead a seminar, entertain on banjo, speak at a banquet, officiate a wedding ceremony, or conduct a funeral. But this was a new experience, and I loved it!

I decided early on not to make my background as a former pastor known if possible, so I just tried to blend in with the crowd as an average visitor. This was like a living lab of church life. I thought it was great fun to walk into a church with no assigned duties, soaking it in, observing, and experiencing new things. I began to appreciate various styles of worship and music, enjoy different program formats, and learn things formerly unknown to me about other denominations.

I soon began to think about how helpful it would have been for me to have had this experience years ago. I could have been a much better pastor. It was changing my perspective in many ways and teaching me things I would never have been aware of otherwise. The desire was taking shape within me to share what I was experiencing with others in ministry.

As I had conversations with my pastor pals during the week, I found their interest level to be very high, and their questions just kept coming. The comments would eventually lead to, "You need to share that with other pastors" or "Write that down, that's good stuff." This scenario has played out the same way repeatedly throughout my mission and continues to this day. Whenever I bring up my church visits, I am bombarded with questions from individuals on every level of church ministry involvement.

THE MAIN PURPOSE EMERGES

The more churches I visited, the more a plan crystallized. I began making notes to record my observations on each church I attended. I had a chance to meet informally with several pastors of churches I had visited, sharing information I learned about their churches, including strong points as well as weaknesses. For the most part, they were receptive and appreciative. This led to additional questions and further discussion.

It was obvious that the information I was gaining had possibilities to make a church stronger and more effective. How could I best share what I was learning with those who wanted and needed to hear it? Maybe I could offer to meet with each pastor and staff to report the findings of my visit to their church. Perhaps holding a seminar for pastors would be the way to go. I wasn't sure. With a growing desire in my heart to support local pastors and be of benefit to the church, my constant prayer was for God to show me how to best use what I was experiencing.

In the meantime, I began developing a system to consistently record details of each church visit. After much analyzing and fine-tuning, I settled on a set of forms to keep track of my data as I continued my weekly church visits.

I finally sensed from the Lord the direction I should go with all this. After completing all my church visits, I would write a letter to all the pastors, explaining what I had been doing as a secret church shopper. I would enclose a written report of what I had experienced at their church and offer to discuss with them further if they cared to call me.

My early church visits, as well as conversations with pastors and staff personnel, had already helped me forge my main purpose: *to provide firsthand information for the church to advance the kingdom of God.*

My plan had solidified, and a project was born. I called it "What in Heaven Is Going On at Church?"

Amen—so be it!

And what about the decision to write a book? Well, that came later. Many people suggested that I write a book, even urged me to write a book. I toyed with the idea. Then a friend, who is a seminary professor, told me, "You've got to write a book. We don't have this kind of information. I'll use it as a textbook in my classes." That did it! I'm an author![1]

---

1   I was asked many times, "Did your wife, Sandy, go with you on your church visits?" The answer is that she was able to go with me for some of the visits, but the majority of the time, I went alone. Sandy teaches an adult Bible study class at our home church on Sunday mornings. So when I was pursuing my secret-church-shopper trek on Sunday mornings, she was faithfully and joyfully fulfilling her teaching obligation.

There were times when she could meet up with me after her class if the church to visit was close enough. A sub filled in for her for a few significant occasions, and Saturday services presented no conflict. For the most part, being alone worked to my advantage in blending in with the crowd. Every Sunday afternoon, I related to my wife detailed accounts of my visit. In this way, she was able to enter into my experience along with me throughout the journey and is my greatest supporter!

2

Let's Visit a Church Together
The Arrival

Let me begin by sharing with you the *visitor routine* I followed in connection with every church visit. Among other things, this helped me to consistently gather the same information about each church.

BEING A SECRET CHURCH SHOPPER

- I prayerfully selected the church to visit one week in advance.
- I viewed the church website and called to verify the service times.
- I arrived at the church twenty-five to thirty minutes early.
- I prayed in the church parking lot that any preconceived ideas and personal prejudices would be removed.
- I parked a good distance from the front door of the church to see if I would be greeted as I approached the entrance.
- I lingered in the lobby/foyer, trying to look like a first-timer.
- I intentionally did not initiate any conversations, waiting instead to be spoken to.
- Upon entering the worship center, I chose a seat in a conspicuously visible location within the first eight to ten rows.
- After the service, I lingered again to see if I would be spoken to.

When a new person drives into a church parking lot, their visiting experience begins. From this moment on, they will be assessing the church and forming opinions about it based on everything they see, hear, and feel. *Everything* they encounter matters! We would expect the music and the sermon to be a big deal, but each detail will play a part in formulating the first-timer's estimation of the church. From the signage to the welcome they experience, the cleanliness of the restrooms, and the availability of coffee—all combine to give a positive or negative feel to the newcomer.

Based on the 115 worship services I attended across 28 denominations, I have compiled a list of components encountered during a church visit. Not all are applicable to all churches, but many are common to all. The following are pertinent to the time of arrival on the church grounds to the beginning of the worship service:

o   Parking lot
o   Signage
o   Bible study classes
o   Welcome desk
o   Coffee shop
o   Ushers
o   Bulletins/other printed handouts
o   Countdown clock

I invite you to go to church with me. Let's hurry—I don't want to be late!

As you encounter each of the components in the above list, look at each through the eyes of a first-time visitor and see how you might feel.

PARKING LOT

Most folks don't give much thought to parking lots. However, it is the first thing a person will experience when visiting a church. Understandably, the size of the lot is nearly always proportional to the size of the church. Many large churches have golf carts and trams to shuttle folks from and to their cars before and after services. Some megachurches have to rely on off-campus parking lots to meet their needs, in which case buses are used to transfer churchgoers back and forth. The advantage to the user is to be picked up right at or near their vehicle and to be dropped off at the preferred entrance to the building.

Most churches have designated parking areas for the handicapped, first-time visitors, and senior adults. I have also observed spots reserved for children's ministry, expectant moms, special needs, the pastor, and sometimes the church staff.

A well-planned and properly marked parking lot with appropriate signage and a parking team is a huge plus to any church of any size. In fact, I would say that it is even crucial. The larger the church, the larger the parking lots, and the greater the need for a top-notch, well-trained parking team. It takes tons of effort in training, supervision, organization, and dedication.

I sincerely believe those serving on a parking team are called to that ministry as much as any church staff member. Responsibilities include directing the flow of traffic, welcoming guests, and assisting handicapped or senior adults. They must arrive at church very early to be prepared. Getting ready may include an organizational meeting and announcements, a time of prayer, donning vests, preparing vehicles, setting out traffic cones and signs before proceeding to man their stations. Then when church is done, all equipment must be retrieved and stored to be ready for next Sunday. Their duties continue no matter what the weather conditions are like.

A word of caution: an adequate number of volunteers is essential for a rotation system to be in place. Otherwise, parking team members will be *at* church every Sunday but never *in* church. This is unacceptable, even if it is the team member's preference. No one should be in a service role that excludes them from participation in corporate worship and Bible study on an ongoing basis.

My Worst Parking Lot Experience

It was an average-size church and had two parking lots, one beside the church and the other directly across the street. Both were asphalt surfaces. The one next to the church was lined to designate where cars were to park. The other was not marked. I arrived early and parked in the back of the lot across the street. It had a single one-lane driveway for entering and exiting. Metal posts with strung wire surrounded the asphalt. Red ribbons were attached to the wire.

The first thing I noticed was the absence of a parking team, which would have been especially helpful in assisting folks to safely cross the street. Since I had arrived early, I did not have a problem parking my car. However, when church was over, I noticed that cars were parked in all kinds of ways because there were no lines to indicate placement. The result of this was a lot of wasted space as people parked wherever and however they chose.

Again, everyone had to navigate across the street on their own. With no one to direct traffic exiting the single-lane driveway onto the busy street—well, it was just a mess. It was frustrating, and it was even dangerous. As I was driving away from the church, I thought, *I would never visit this church again.* That is what other visitors will think too. Come to think of it, the parking-lot experience was just a sample of the remainder of the visiting experience.

My Best Parking Lot Experience

As I drove into the parking lot of this large church, there was a big sign on my right that read, "First-time visitors, please turn on your blinkers." I did, and as I continued, a man wearing a brightly colored vest and headset waved at me to stop. He was quite personable and friendly. We introduced ourselves, and he directed me to the designated visitors lot. As I approached the visitors lot, another man, wearing a different colored vest, waved at me and directed me where to park.

As I got out of the car, he said, "Welcome, Buddy, we are happy to have you here today" (he knew my name because the first man told him—remember the headset?). He asked if he could escort me to the front door, and I agreed. As we walked, many people greeted me with a word or hand wave. The vest color of my host was an indication to members that I was a first-timer. He introduced me to the greeter at the door, who took me to the visitors desk where I received a visitor packet and a ticket for a free cup of coffee at the snack bar.

I was warmly greeted on every hand. The gracious lady at the visitors desk introduced me to another person, who invited me to take a brief tour of the facility. I accepted the invitation, and he guided me around the building, and we ended up in the worship center. He courteously told me that I could sit anywhere I chose. As he pointed to different areas in the auditorium, he made comments about which section is known to be rather cold or loud or whatever. I selected where I wanted to sit. He escorted me there, and as I approached, he introduced me by name to some folks who were already seated nearby. Again, I was warmly welcomed by all. As he departed, he said, "Buddy, I will be right back there"—he pointed— "if you need anything."

When the service was over, I was exiting and ran into my gracious host, who greeted me yet another time. He even remembered my name! On the way out, I was spoken to by several in the lobby. I returned to the visitors desk and was given a really nice-quality large coffee mug. As I departed the building, more friendly greetings were received, and this continued as I made my way to the parking lot. As I was driving off the property, I passed a sign that read, "Thank you for coming. You are welcome anytime! God bless you!"

That same evening, I received a welcome call from the church. Two days later, I received a personal letter from the pastor and, in three days, a handwritten card from the lady at the visitors desk. This kind of stuff does not just happen! It takes hours of planning, training, dedication, and an army of committed folks. But what an impact it makes on a first-time guest!

Later on, I called the church and talked to the person in charge of this ministry just to express my thanks. We talked for about forty minutes, and he explained how obviously dedicated their church was to treating every visitor the way I had been hosted. They have regular training sessions and over 250 rotating volunteers on the visitors team. He shared with me that they put that kind of effort into this ministry because they want visitors to "sense they are loved, feel welcome, and come to know Christ as their Savior." Amen to that!

In the case of this particular church, the parking-lot experience was a foretaste of the overall church ministry. First impressions count!

SIGNAGE

Church signage falls into two categories: exterior and interior. It is very frustrating to drive into a church property and not know where to go. The larger the campus, the greater the difficulty.

Like most church members who have become familiar with their church property because they attend regularly, I never thought much about signs either—that is, until I walked into 115 different church buildings for the first time and tried to navigate my way. It is surprising to find so many churches lacking in this area. Visitors being able to easily find their way around is important!

In addition to parking-lot signage mentioned previously, here are some examples of exterior signage that would be helpful for new people. There should be signs in parking lots and/or walkways to indicate direction of the following:

- Worship center
- Preschool/children's area
- Youth area
- Senior-adult area

There should also be signs on building over entrances to the following:

- Activities building
- Worship center
- Chapel
- A name for each entrance (*North Entrance* or *South, East, West*, or other designated name for entrance)

A few examples of interior signage are the following:

- Restrooms
- Worship center
- Chapel
- Fellowship hall
- Bookstore
- Library
- Prayer room
- Connection center
- Classrooms (room numbers)

Signs must be done very well to produce the desired results. Gone are the days of poster board and felt-tip markers! Only professionally made signs should be considered. They can be quite expensive and are difficult to change or adjust once installed. Therefore, decisions regarding permanent signage should be made by qualified people spending adequate time and prayer in the process to determine location of signs and what they are to indicate.

Churches need to have good-quality signs that have the following characteristics:

- Easily visible and strategically located
- Printed with large clear fonts
- Located just inside each entrance and in obvious high-traffic areas

- Easy to read and understand
- Installed at heights that are above the crowds
- In hallways mounted perpendicular to the wall to be easily read at a distance from either direction

Quality signs are not just a good idea—they are vital! Here is an example of a sign I found in a church. It was located on the wall outside the fellowship hall.

Come And Join Us This Week
…something for everyone!!
7–8:30 p.m. 1st & 3rd Mondays—Youth Praise Dancers
7–8:30 p.m. 2nd & 4th Mondays—Adult Praise Dancers
6:30 p.m.—Tuesday Nights: Family Night
6:30 p.m. Tuesdays—9:00 Saturdays before
3rd Sundays—Hands in Ministry
8:00 p.m. Tuesday—Male Chorus—Three Tuesdays before the 4th

There were ten more events listed on this sign. To me, this is TMI, confusing, and difficult to read. Perhaps it served a useful purpose to the members, but from a visitor's perspective, it was way too much information.

Signage should primarily be geared for guests. The lack of adequate signage and/or quality of signage will make an impression on new people—aim for a positive impression!

GREETERS

The greeters who work the doors of a church offer a second chance to make a good impression (the first chance is the parking lot). A sincere smile and warm greeting in a friendly voice with full eye contact are standard tools for extending an effective welcome.

Greeters should be mature enough to handle their responsibilities and young enough to inject energy and sincerity into their approach. In fact, I would go so far as to say having enthusiastic young adults serve as greeters is a real plus. The typical age of folks in this role seems to be fifty or sixty and above in most churches. It is understandable that older adults with no young children to deal with on Sunday mornings are more available to arrive early at their post. But the greeters represent the face of the church. Even if the senior adults enlisted are wonderfully personable, it is highly appealing to young adults to be welcomed by people of their own age-group. If at all possible, strive for a variety of ages among the greeters at the front door. And if Mr. Scowl-On-His-Face volunteers, try to graciously find an alternate role of service for him to fulfill!

None of this just happens—it requires intentionality. A dedicated leader must coordinate the ministry; and folks must be trained, prayed up, and ready to reflect the love of Jesus to everyone who walks in the door. Greeters should be ready to answer FAQs from visitors or at least know how to guide the newcomer to the answer.

As I visited a particular megachurch in my familiar role as a secret church shopper, I found the parking-lot experience to be satisfactory and noticed first-class signs posted in all the right places. As I walked in the front door, three greeters were talking among themselves about the NCAA basketball tournament.

My entrance through the door did not deter them at all from their conversation. None of them looked at me nor said a word to me as one mechanically handed me a bulletin. Little did I know that was a preview of what the entire morning would be like. No one spoke to me during the entire visit except at the designated greet-your-neighbor time in the worship service. When bad things like that happen, I always think, *What if I were a lost and hurting person and really needed help?*

Some larger churches designate greeter team members to circulate among attendees as lobby greeters too, which is nice. The truth of the matter is, all church members should be considered visitor greeters. A simple campaign to raise awareness of this need among the regulars would be invaluable. If fact, I have visited churches where the people at large were so intentionally friendly to me that I would suspect it was a special emphasis of the church leadership.

As a full-time minister, I thought I knew the importance of having trained, well-prepared greeters and ushers. I found that I did realize this fact in theory, but not on a practical level. I have attended numerous staff meetings and been involved in conversations about the myriad aspects and duties of greeting teams, recruitment plans, and training procedures. I have even served with a team of fellow staffers and volunteers to develop a comprehensive strategy for irresistibly welcoming every individual who walked in our doors. It's not that I wasn't convinced that this is vitally important. But now, as a secret church shopper, the real impact hit home as I experienced the good, bad, and ugly of it.

No other ministry in the entire church is in a position to meet and greet visitors and guests as they walk in the doors of the church. The greeting team has the responsibility to set the mood for these folks. Some statistics report that most first-timers will form a lasting view of the church within eight minutes of walking in the door.

The low point of all my visits occurred in churches where I walked into the church, sat through the service, and walked back to my car without a single person saying a word to me or acknowledging my existence in any way whatsoever. Being completely ignored while surrounded by presumably Christian people is not a good feeling. I had this experience in more than a few churches. How can the church wave the flag of "Jesus loves you, and so do we" and behave in such a manner?

I made this query of a church leader who called me twenty-three days after I visited their church. The reply I received was, "Oh, we were just having a bad day." No church can afford to have this kind of "bad day" even once. I always look at this kind of situation from the standpoint of a visitor who really needs to be loved and cared for. Would you come back if this happened to you? No doubt about it, earning an A+ in this area takes vision, hard work, recruiting, training, consistency, and prayer. Is it worth it? To do less is inexcusable!

Greeters are afforded an opportunity to share God's love, one person right after the other as they walk in the doors of the church. They are the first touch of the church. They must be trained to greet, direct people to what they need, and do it lovingly every Sunday. Anytime they meet a guest or visitor, they are shouting in a loud, silent voice, *How I treat you is just a sample of how much our Lord loves you.*

With every church visit, I always followed the same routine so I could get the same information about each church. One part of my standard operating procedure was that I did not initiate any conversations, waiting instead to be spoken to. When visitors are not spoken to or warmly greeted, they do not take their calendars and circle the upcoming Sunday and write, "Be sure to go back to this church."

The meeting, greeting, welcoming, shaking hands, hosting, smiling—all in the name of Jesus—are vital. Can you believe this? In forty-seven out of one hundred churches, I was spoken to by one or more people to some degree or other. In the remaining fifty-three churches, not one person spoke a word to me!

BIBLE STUDY CLASSES

It is interesting to read the history of Sunday schools. In the very early years, American churches took on the responsibility of providing general education for children because there were so few schools, especially in rural areas. In fact, the actual name *Sunday school* was born from this concept. This is a great example of the church stepping up to meet human needs.

Sunday morning Bible study classes are an integral part of most churches today. In some cases, they meet on another day of the week and often in homes. The term *Sunday school* is still around; but more often, other names are used, such as *small groups, grow groups, focus time, huddle teams, connection classes,* or *fellowship groups,* to list a few. They commonly gather to study the Bible and other facets of Christianity on a weekly basis and are led by a teacher, discussion leader, or facilitator of some sort, based on the style of study.

The primary purpose of Bible study is obviously foundational to carrying out the great commission Jesus issued to all in the family of God. We are instructed to "make disciples, teaching them to observe all that I have commanded you." There it is—teaching all of God's Word! We as the church must not neglect this very basic responsibility!

There are secondary advantages to Bible study groups. Folks need to meet new people, develop relationships, and spend time together to know and be known. It is nearly impossible to do this when the only church involvement is worship-service attendance. This is a *huge* need today. Our fast-paced, high-tech society tends to isolate people.

Everyone needs to find the small church within the large church where they can connect on a personal level. Even in small or average-sized churches, no one can be really close friends with an entire congregation. The small group is where personal problems and needs can be shared and friends can minister to one another through prayer and in other practical ways. Even Jesus led a small group—we call them the disciples!

I visited a number of churches where the major focus is on the worship service, and no small-group Bible studies are offered. This usually meant a lengthy (sometimes two-hour) time of worship, which was often glorious. However, I believe it is a disservice to the membership to omit the opportunity afforded by small-group Bible studies.

There was a time that nearly every church used some type of Bible-study materials produced by their denomination. These publications were sometimes called *quarterlies* because a new one came out every three months. The idea was to have everyone in the church or denomination studying the same age-appropriate lessons. This still exists in some denominations. It appears that smaller churches are more likely to use these resources.

However, today, churches are no longer tied to these denominationally produced materials. There is a plethora of wonderful options available. The huge variety of top-notch courses produced by independent publishers, as well as denominational agencies, is almost overwhelming. The difficulty is not to find adequate material but to narrow the selection.

There are still highly gifted teachers with sufficient Bible knowledge to develop their own teaching materials. And many of them do an excellent job of teaching Bible truth directly from the Bible without the use of a printed curriculum. However, abundant resources can easily be found online and in Christian bookstores to effectively enhance Bible learning. There are self-guided study books with suggested discussion questions as well as video teaching. Many well-known Bible teachers and preachers have written and/or video-recorded excellent lessons.

Most of the churches I visited that included Bible study groups of some kind offered a wide range of options for adults. Studying God's Word is of utmost importance. Second Timothy 2:15 cannot be taken lightly: "Study to show yourself approved."

WELCOME DESK

The welcome desk could also be called the welcome center, but the most common name I found to be used was connection center. In fact, the word *connect* or *connection* seems to be the latest buzzword around church life.

It is best if the welcome desk is centrally located and easily seen upon entering the building. Everything that is true of greeters as pertains to a warm and friendly welcome and training would naturally apply to those who serve at the welcome desk. Volunteers should be able to answer typical questions a visitor might ask. Generally, I have found their main purpose to be to direct newcomers where to find classrooms for all ages and to provide first-timers with a welcome gift of some kind either before or after the worship service.

My number one recommendation is—whatever you do, have someone on duty at all times! I have visited churches who directed me to their welcome desk only to find it empty of a live human being. This is *information central* and must be maintained and staffed with efficient, well-trained, personable, and dedicated volunteers.

COFFEE SHOP

Almost all churches serve coffee. I have seen coffee bars in churches that have ranged from two coffeepots on a table with a leaning stack of Styrofoam cups and a handwritten sign, attached to the wall with tape, that read, "Donations appreciated for coffee," to setups that would rival Starbucks and other commercial endeavors. And some actually serve Starbucks-brand coffee as well as other gourmet types. Coffee bars have been given names like the 2nd Cup (guess where I saw that one!), Holy Grounds, the Garden of Eatin', and Muddy Waters, just to name a few. They are nice to have—certainly not a necessity (some might dispute that) but popular among most churchgoers. Often, donuts and other pastries are offered too. Sometimes all is offered complimentary, sometimes donations are requested, and sometimes specific charges are required just like any commercial business.

Important here is to assure cleanliness and proper maintenance of the coffee station. Food prep and proper handling is serious business and should be managed accordingly. If it is not self-service, the coffee bar should be manned by the same type of personalities with the same training required for greeters. This may be just coffee, but it is a reflection of the entire church ministry and must be done with excellence.

USHERS

What is the purpose of an usher? In my estimation, an usher would be helpful if the auditorium is so filled that finding an empty seat is difficult or if the service is already in progress. I have been in a few services of a more formal nature where I have walked in to sit down and have been stopped by an usher, told when I could proceed, and then ushered to a specific seat of their choosing when there were plenty available. I am of the opinion that people want the freedom to choose their own seating location and not be told where they have to sit.

Although the above is the exception rather than the rule (PTL for that!), I have also encountered several ushers who could easily fall into the grumpy-old-man category. I have had ushers who made me feel more like I was attending a funeral service than a worship service. It would be nice if someone could teach them to at least *smile*! This is another role that would best be filled by outgoing, cheerful personalities!

BULLETINS/OTHER PRINTED HANDOUTS

At every church I visited, I made sure to pick up at least two bulletins, which I then used to record tons of notes. The information would later be transferred to the church evaluation form (CEF), which was part of my system to record data about each church visit. I have collected dozens of bulletins of every kind, shape, configuration, and style. As would be expected, those from churches with a more traditional form of worship included an order of service, listing each item on the program, hymn titles, sermon titles, etc. As previously mentioned, the bulletin for certain liturgical worship formats included every word spoken by the priest/pastor and every word of response by the congregation.

Generally speaking, most other churches used the printed bulletin strictly for announcements and promo of activities rather than an order of service. A surprising number gave out no printed bulletin whatsoever. In a few churches with younger congregations, the bulletin was digitally accessed on smartphones and tablets, which will surely gain in popularity. Already, younger adults rely heavily on websites and digital media for announcements rather than the usual printed flyers.

Many pastors include a fill-in-the-blanks sermon outline or teaching guide in the bulletin. This can be a good practice if it focuses the hearer's attention and enhances their learning of truth. Otherwise, it is a wasted effort. The most memorable guide I received had seventy-three blanks to fill in, and many of the blanks required multiword answers. The pastor lost me about halfway through his message!

The largest bulletin I received had fourteen pages and listed forty-three components to their order of service. Another contained ads that were sold to various businesses (described elsewhere in this book).

The bulletins that seem to be the most popular are very simple. One of my favorites is from a church that specifically reaches out to the unchurched. A 9 × 12 sheet of heavy card stock was folded in half to form four brightly colored printed pages. The reader's attention is easily drawn to the up-to-date graphics on each side. The front page reads, "Welcome to _____ Church" and contains their logo.

The inside left says, "Welcome to _____" and then four colorful panels titled with the following list:

1. Relax
2. Drop off the kids
3. Fill out the card
4. Grab a free gift

These four boxes contain colorful, real-life photos. The inside right reads,

What to expect:

1. Our band will play five songs
2. Someone will pray and say "Hi"

3. A pastor will do a talk
4. There will be a closing song
5. Someone will say "Bye,"...after 60 minutes, it's over!

I timed their service, and it was over in exactly fifty-eight minutes. The back read, "Fellowship 5"—the top five announcements you need to know. (Five announcements were listed and briefly described.)

Church bulletins are just that, church bulletins. Yes, there could even be a few bloopers added to those we all know and love. But I also discovered lists of dos and don'ts and various reminders aimed at the attendees. The most common do was, "Turn off your cell phones." The most frequent don't was, "Don't forget to turn off your cell phones." Get the point?

The following is a list of other requests, comments, directives, statements, and instructions I discovered in bulletins. I am neither endorsing nor denouncing any of these—I'm just sharing what I saw. Each is printed here exactly as it appeared in the bulletin.

- Be real, be kind, seek beauty, seek God, be hospitable and serve others.
- Stop by the Welcome Center and say "Hello."
- Available is a "Wiggle Room" for families with young children where a live-feed of the service can be seen.
- Large print hymnals and bulletins are available from any usher.
- Visitors, please fill out the sheet in the Friendship Pad when it is passed.
- At all times, but especially during services, one should remember that one is in the house of God.
- No perfect people allowed.
- Leave your card, we promise no one will bother you at home!
- Please use the Quiet Room for consistently crying babies.
- Respect for the Word of God requires good manners and poise, therefore, please avoid any talking or unnecessary

movement that would distract serious students of the Word of God.

- We will hold a toiletry collection for the Prison Ministry.
- Our Girl Scouts are expanding. We have a new group of Daiseys joining.
- All formal members are urged to attend the 6PM business meeting.
- We do not consider ourselves better than any other church, however, we are different.
- We want to keep Jesus Christ the same and change the wrapping paper.
- This bulletin includes icons to alert worshippers of the bodily attitude to be taken in divine service.[1]
- Please feel free to sing in Spanish or English, standing or sitting.
- Make sure your children go to the restrooms before the service…please!
- Our children deserve to play, study, sleep and live their lives without the fear of intruders harming them or the orphanage's possessions. Help us raise funds needed for adequate playground and adequate fence.[2]
- As communion trays are passed down each row, please take a wafer and juice, replace the empty cup in the tray and pass it to the next guest.
- 6:30–7:30PM—cocktail hour & cash only bar.[3]
- Due to budgetary reasons the Hospitality Desk will be closed except from 8AM to noon on Saturdays.
- We operate on your support! You may be led to give into fertile soil.
- Reverence and good manners are required.

---

1   There are sitting and standing icons.

2   I have no explanation of what is being referenced.

3   This refers to an upcoming Saturday evening event.

- Today is Popsicle Sunday! Cool off with a popsicle and stay for Sunday School.
- No irrelevant conversations should take place in the narthex or in any part of the church.
- We encourage you to notice the names of those around you and greet them by name.
- You are welcome to take this brochure with you
- Please sign-up now! (Hint: If you do it now, you get your choice of times.)
- If you are a guest, take an opportunity to introduce yourself to us.
- Whenever the Priest is facing the people or outside the altar, everyone should stand still wherever they are.
- Please wait for the Deacons to dismiss.
- Before you drop-out or cop-out, discover your potential in Sunday School.
- Change your "scars to stars" and quit your "stinking thinking."
- The wearing of shorts is NOT permitted.
- Only baptized or chrismated orthodox Christians who are in good standing with the church are permitted to receive Holy Communion.
- Ladies are asked to remove their lipstick prior to receiving Holy Communion.
- We want you to know about different things that can happen in the church and where it can be found in the Bible.
- Are you in? IN-volved, IN-gaged, IN-vested?
- Strollers are not allowed in the sanctuary.
- Rodeo Day is next week—we encourage you to dress western...just keep it modest.
- The best way to know about our church is to just "jump-in!"
- We call ourselves a "Church For The Un-churched," we exist to reach people who don't normally attend services.

There are more, but I think you have had enough!

Part of my secret-church-shopper operational procedure was to pick up various printed materials that are readily available to all. Additional printed resources were always of value to me for learning more about the church. As I was exiting a church known for their liberal theological views and disdain for evangelical churches, I picked up a copy of their monthly newsletter from a table by the door.

Their newsletter contained the following article under the title of "Religious Education Curriculum":

> Once again fall is upon us and we are planning our educational program for our children. This year we've decided to face a perennial problem: our children facing fundamentalist, evangelical and Pentecostal peers who like to spout the Bible as if they have a corner on truth, embarrassing our children and provoking feelings of ignorance and inferiority. We've decided to hit the problem head on. We're going to teach Judeo-Christian literature. But you need not be alarmed. It's amazing how liberally and humanistically this literature can be taught. Actually, the Christian Bible is a liberal book and it is truly appalling what conservatives do to it. With their liberalistic and legalistic orientation, the book becomes a disgusting mass of mythology that no thinking person can swallow. We, the churches Religious Education Committee, think it's time to face this problem rather than run away from it. The Bible, along with Greek philosophy, Roman government structure and law, and Germanic cultural forms, have forged the basis of our modern western literature to our children, presenting our churches values and commitment to modern world views, while tooling our children to take a back seat to none when it comes to "rightly dividing the word of truth." Rest assured! We are not "Bible thumpers." We're simply not going to be on the defensive any more. It has been said, "The best defense is a good offense." One of our major humanist values is use of intellect in matters of religion. It is a crying shame if we educate our children

in every other area but leave them ignorant about Judeo-Christian literature. That leaves a vacuum in their education that others are sitting in the wings waiting to fill. Many young people have expressed with anger how their church and/or their parents have let them down by not exposing them to our understanding of these stories and histories. No more! We will appreciate your help and support, while we tackle this need head on as a _____ church!

This article verifies several things to me:

1. There is a spiritual war going on, and evangelical Christians are right in the middle of it.
2. Some so-called churches are not teaching the truth of the gospel of Jesus Christ.
3. Without God, man has a depraved mind and drifts further and further from the truth.

COUNTDOWN CLOCK

These are really a nice touch to a church schedule. Large digital clocks, usually located in the foyer and projected on the screens in the worship center, count down the time, second by second, until the worship service starts. The purpose, of course, is to get everyone into the worship center and seated by the time the service begins. It is a very effective tool.

Some churches place the countdown clocks throughout the entire facility in obvious, high-traffic areas. Most of the ones I have seen start their countdown at ten minutes—others at five minutes. A *must* is that when it reads 0:00, the service starts instantly. If it doesn't, it is a huge letdown, and the clock becomes meaningless. When this happens, it is a lot like kissing a girl through a screen door—there's nothing much to it!

3

Let's Visit a Church Together
The Service Begins

The worship service as a whole is undoubtedly the most important part of a church program. Any visitor will be especially alert to how each phase of the service is presented. Allow me to share with you my observations from 100+ church visits to learn how others do church. Here are the areas of focus at this stage of the visit:

- Media/screens
- Music
- Welcoming guests
- The Bible
- Corporate prayer
- Children's sermons/children's church/childcare

MEDIA/SCREENS

Advances in media technology have played a huge role in the average church experience today. Even among smaller churches, it is common to have quality sound equipment and special lighting capabilities. Almost all churches have large screens to project words to songs and other elements of the service.

Most large churches have full-time media personnel and high expectations of media quality for every presentation. Megachurches with state-of-the-art media capabilities rival those of professional music superstars and their concerts.

Media, used well, can greatly enhance the experience of worship, without a doubt. However, some feel we may have created a monster! The average churchgoer doesn't realize how many trained technicians are required to put on a regular weekly worship service. Paid personnel, as well as highly trained volunteers, are typically run ragged to cover the media needs for a week's worth of meetings and activities. Yet we have become accustomed to the high degree of professionalism and would be disappointed to do without it. If the high tech were missing, some members would be too.

What would happen in a high-tech church when the power goes off? Could we still have church? (PTL for backup emergency power systems!)

I have visited churches where the use of graphics and video in a multimedia presentation were absolutely breathtaking! The sound, the music, the visuals all come together to lift the spirit heavenward in worship and praise. I have also been present in services where I felt like a spectator to a glitzy showbiz production and not a participant at all. What makes the difference? That will be discussed further under the next heading about music.

We can expect that the use of media technology in the church is here to stay. It is another great tool for magnifying the Lord Jesus Christ in worship—we must make sure it is used for that purpose and not merely to entertain.

MUSIC

Since I visited one hundred plus churches, ranging in size from thirty-five to fifty thousand plus members, in twenty-eight different denominations, I heard, saw, experienced, enjoyed, participated in, worshiped, and sang with all types of music presentations. Some of the music was just great, some good, some tolerable, some fair, and some just plain bad. Being a musician—some folks tell me, "You're not a musician, you're a banjo player," but that is beside the point—I do know enough about music to recognize when a band is prepared or not. I do know when their instruments are in tune or not, and I do know about the lead, rhythm, and harmony aspects of music.

Because I always arrived early at the churches I attended, I had many opportunities to witness and hear worship teams and musicians making sound checks and final preparations for their Sunday services. Two things became obvious:

1. Some were highly prepared and were just putting the finishing touches on their musical presentations.
2. Some were not prepared at all and were scrambling to get it together at the last minute.

Music presented in church (or any ministry) must be to the best of their ability because it has eternal results, and it is a love offering to Him. Shabby, poorly prepared musical presentations have no business in churches.

I relate the following true story to illustrate how people have different attitudes about music and/or musical instruments used in church. I was invited to preach in a church that was about 150 miles from Houston and was looking forward to the trip and experience. When I arrived at 10:00 a.m. for the 11:00 a.m. service, I walked into the worship center, carrying my Bible in one hand and my banjo case in the other.

No one said a word to me, so I said to a man standing nearby, "I need to See Mr. So-and-So" (not his real name). He was the person who had invited me, and I had only talked to him by phone. The man I had inquired from left to find Mr. So-and-So. When Mr. So-and-So appeared, I extended my hand and introduced myself. He responded to me by pointing at my banjo case and saying, "What is that?" I explained, "It is a banjo, and I am going to play a medley of gospel tunes that relate to my sermon." He abruptly said, "We don't play banjos in our church." He continued to speak as he turned toward the back of the church and pointed to a large clock on the wall and said, "We also get out at five minutes to twelve." That was the extent of our conversation.

The service started at eleven sharp. The announcements, congregational singing, and choir special were presented, and I preached. At 11:55 a.m., it was over, and I was through. I will never know why Mr. So-and-So was so opposed to my banjo.

In the dozens of churches I attended, I have experienced all types of music. Orchestras with magnificent instrumentation, two-hundred-plus-voice choirs, praise bands, a cappella groups, guitars (acoustical and electric, six-string and twelve-string), pianos, keyboards, electronic organs, pipe organs, synthesizers, drums, banjos (four-string and five-string), ukuleles (all four types), drums, drum machines, mandolins, harmonicas, fiddles, and tambourines have all been part of the musical presentations.

In Psalm 150, all these instruments are mentioned in some form or other—if you use your imagination. I believe any instrument and any type of vocal group can be used to praise and glorify God and share his eternal, loving message. God can be praised and honored through a variety of styles of music too. Many people have their preferences, but in my opinion, that is just what they are—preferences.

With today's huge advances in technology, sound, visuals, and special effects, the music possibilities are unlimited. The music in any church should be used to honor Jesus, enhance the worship experience, spiritually inspire the congregation, and prepare the way for the message to be presented boldly and clearly. Any music ministry would do well to utilize all the creativity they can muster in using their full technical capabilities. The result can be dynamite!

However, the focus of the music is to add to the worship experience, not detract from it. Music in churches is not show business; it is Jesus business—that is why it must be first-class. Worship pastors, choirs, musicians, praise bands, accompanists, sound technicians, and the entire worship team should all be prayed up and spiritually ready to present the best music possible for the glory and honor of our Lord. Whether it's one guitar or a 250-voice choir and orchestra, all should be prayed up, practiced up, tuned up, and prepared to honor our Lord with the best music possible every time.

Where is the fine line that separates music that is truly uplifting and worshipful from music that is routine and empty? What makes the difference? Is it talent? Technology? Creativity? Adequate planning?

All those are important, but it goes beyond that. Here's my opinion. Nothing and no one sets the stage for worship in a church service as much as the worship leader himself. As goes the worship leader, so goes the service. That's a lot of responsibility to lay on one individual—only through the power of the Holy Spirit within can this be achieved.

I have seen obviously talented and highly trained singers flawlessly lead a service, but they seem shallow, mechanical, and self-centered. It became a performance. I have also seen dedicated guys with humble spirits and loving demeanors seem obviously filled with the Spirit of God and able to lift the congregation to worship at the feet of Jesus. It must come from a close, personal, and consistent walk with Christ. A leader may be able to fake it occasionally, but over time, the truth will show through. From this standpoint, technology is merely incidental—genuine worship can happen with it or without it.

I have attended cowboy church services wearing boots and jeans in dusty barns as fiddles, guitars, and banjos were used to honor our Lord with a country-Western flare. I have sat reverently, wearing a suit and tie, in stately churches with highly trained and talented choirs singing the traditional hymns of the faith from a hymnbook (no words on a screen). I have been thrilled by the congregational a cappella singing in magnificent harmony in churches that used no musical instruments.

I have participated in services led by lively praise bands using contemporary worship songs with many worshipers clapping their hands or lifting them high in adoration of the Lord. All were worshipful experiences. All were honest expressions of praise offered to the God of the universe. I believe all were acceptable to God when expressed from a pure and grateful heart. I have a confession to make—personally, I love it all!

When chatting with a pastor of a cowboy church about music in today's churches, he told me, "The soup is the same. The bowl is just different." (Soup is the message of our Lord Jesus Christ. The bowl is the way it is presented.)

I am saddened to say there is still a lingering attitude around some churches that is a carryover from the worship wars that began when contemporary music was introduced. By and large, the senior-adult community disliked and/or disapproved of the new style that featured praise bands and new songs with lyrics projected on a large screen. I lived through that era and think I have an understanding of the perspectives of both sides.

I was senior-adult pastor (before I was a full-fledged senior adult myself) to a group of folks who were deeply wounded by the attitudes expressed to them by younger proponents of contemporary music. I dealt with my parents and my wife's parents who were also deeply affected. These were all good people faced with making a huge adjustment in their church life. They grieved the loss of the beloved hymns they had held near and dear for all their lives. A transition to something entirely foreign to their concept of church music was difficult. Many rebelled and became embittered. Others moved to different churches where the trend toward contemporary music had not yet taken hold. Sadly, many dropped out altogether.

The younger generation who espoused the contemporary style largely viewed the opposition as just grouchy old fuddy-duddies who needed to "get a life." Seldom were feelings considered or resistance handled with understanding or gracious diplomacy. Decisions to go with the new way were made by leadership with little or no regard for the will of the old-timers. The casualties of these wars that should never have been were great and are a disgrace to the body of Christ. Many pastors lived to regret their handling (or nonhandling) of the issues. In hindsight, it would seem that if proper care had been exercised and explanations had been lovingly communicated, perhaps a satisfactory bridge could have been built to better make the transition.

But here we are in the present with a contemporary style of worship music being the most prevalent (or at least what is sometimes called a blended style). There are still some disgruntled senior adults lingering in the shadows; but most have either graduated to heaven, surrendered to the inevitable, or selflessly joined the younger crowd in embracing contemporary music. Contemporary music is not going away anytime soon—this is a case of "if you can't beat 'em, join 'em!"

One church-wide "holdout" regarding contemporary music is an average-to-small-sized church I visited. Their exterior signage, weekly bulletin, and even a freeway billboard all declare, "We preach from the Bible and sing from the hymnbook!" To someone who knows anything at all about music disagreements among the brethren, that byline seems to carry a bit of an attitude with it.

My suspicion was confirmed. That is exactly what I heard expressed in personal conversations with several members when I visited—they were quite adamant. The first half of that description is certainly commendable, but if they stick with the second half, they will likely be able to count down to their extinction one funeral at a time.[1]

I offer here some suggestions—with an earnest prayer that we "fervently love one another from the heart," as admonished by Peter (1 Peter 1:22).

The following is to be read only by those age sixty and above:

- Rejoice in the number of young families that are being brought into the fellowship of your church because they are attracted to the contemporary music.

---

1   There was a noticeable absence of young people in attendance.

- Bless the younger generation by your joyful acceptance of "their" music as your personal sacrifice to God. They will love you for it.
- Resist the temptation to complain and verbally express your criticism of the contemporary music ministry. Keep negative comments to yourself. You won't change anything except their opinion of you.
- Support the music ministry with your prayers.
- Never send e-mails to pastors and church staff unless they are words of praise and encouragement.
- Some folks find it helpful to stuff tissues in their ears when the music is too loud. Be thankful if you wear hearing aids—you can turn them off.
- Take advantage of opportunities to enjoy your personal music preference by listening to CDs, certain Christian radio stations, and the Internet.

The following is to be read only by those age fifty-nine and below:

- Be mindful that the senior adults of today are the faithful ones through whom God built the church of yesteryear that you are now enjoying. They deserve your thanks and respect.
- Resist the temptation to speak of negative senior adults in a critical way—better to keep your thoughts to yourself.
- Seek understanding of the feelings of older people. An undesirable style of music may come into vogue and replace your beloved contemporary style when you are a senior adult.
- Honor the senior adults of your church for their dedication and many years of service.
- Leadership, deal with a critic (of any age) by showering them with the genuine love of Jesus through you. Your worst enemy may just become your best supporter! (I've had it happen!)
- Leadership, remove the blinders that focus your attention solely on your musical preference. Consider including a

variety of styles in your overall program—it may enrich the worship experience for everyone. True corporate worship is not dependent on the latest style.

- Leadership, consider a compromise of sorts by turning down the volume a notch or two. When the music is loud enough to produce serious ear pain and a rattling chest, it's pretty difficult to focus on worship! Thankfully I encountered this degree of volume in only a few churches.

Here are a few sidenotes to all:

- The music of the New Testament churches probably differed from any of today's styles.
- The book of Revelation speaks of a "new song" being sung before the Lamb (Rev. 5:9) and a "new song" being sung before the throne (Rev. 14:3). Do you think when we get to heaven we might be surprised by the style of the song? Whatever style it may be, I'm going to love it!
- Many of the melodies of today's well-loved hymns were familiar bar-and-tavern tunes back in the day with Christian words added. These were initially shunned by the faithful for church use but obviously survived their early reputation.
- Even the use of organ music in church was originally considered scandalous by many. The story is told of an incident in the early days of a 175-year-old church, now a vibrant megachurch. Early in their history, when an organ was first acquired, there were those among the membership who opposed the "worldly" addition. The offensive organ mysteriously disappeared from the sanctuary—and was later found floating in the nearby bayou!

My, my, these times, they are a'changin'!

WELCOMING GUESTS

I can well remember back in the day when it was standard practice to ask all visitors in the worship service to stand so they could be recognized and welcomed. Ushers then came forward and handed the guests a visitor's card to fill out. The card usually included a small red ribbon with a straight pin or a red sticker to be attached to their clothing to identify them as visitors so that the members could greet them after the service.

Then came the seeker-sensitive movement, and we discovered that this practice was considered embarrassing by visitors. They didn't like being singled out of the crowd and instead felt more comfortable remaining in the background and unidentified. Not wanting what was intended to be a friendly gesture to be a turnoff to those we were trying to reach, a new approach was established.

Members were asked to stand, and guests were asked to remain seated so that members could meet and greet them. Maybe this idea was a little better. However, I had neighbors at the time who regularly visited our church but never joined. They told me, "We don't want people to know we're visiting, so we just stand with everybody else." Oh well—so much for that idea! Later on, and continuing into our present time, it is more likely to have *everyone* stand and "greet those around you," which includes guests, members, and regular attenders.

During my church-visiting project, I have encountered multiple ways for visitors to be greeted that run the gamut from no acknowledgement whatsoever to over-the-top, focused, right-in-the-spotlight attention on those present in the service for the first time.

Beginning at the lower end of the spectrum—yes, there are actually church services where no mention is made of visitors at all. Next step-up is a simple yet warm greeting verbalized from the worship leader or pastor. Folks are sometimes asked to fill out a visitor's card found either in the pew rack or as a bulletin insert or bulletin tear-off section. Guests may or may not be asked to stand. Sometimes an invitation is extended to meet the pastor in a designated area after the service, where they are often given a free gift of some kind.

Here are some other demonstrations of welcome that I experienced:

- At a very large megachurch with a highly organized and trained army of greeters and ushers, visitors are seated in a reserved front section of the huge auditorium. During the service, the pastor draws attention to this section as he warmly delivers a message of welcome to them.
- The pastor of another church asked all visitors to stand. I stood along with some others present that day. He then asked questions to each individual visitor as a fast-moving usher quickly appeared to hold a mic to speak into—questions such as, What is your name? Do you live in this area? How did you know about our church? Although the intent was to show personal interest in each person, it had a rather awkward feel. Some responders were obviously uncomfortable being put on the spot in such a manner.
- On another occasion, the pastor asked all visitors to stand. He gave a warm welcome, affirmed by the applause of the congregation. He then asked the visitors to lift their hands, "wave at me so I can see you—now reach down and get an offering envelope from the holder on the back of the pew." I did so. He then told us to hold it up in the air. I followed instructions, thinking that he was going to pray for the offering. He then said, "We expect all visitors and guests to give a minimum $5 offering!" Whoa! I didn't see that coming! A short time later, when everybody filed by the offering basket on a table in the front of the auditorium, my envelope was completed as instructed!
- This one wins the prize for unique visitor welcome of the decade! The pastor asked all visitors to stand. He then

emphasized how happy he and his church were to have visitors. So far, that was pretty standard procedure for welcoming folks. What happened next was definitely not the norm.

He asked the entire congregation to join the visitors in standing and then said, "Now, church, let's show our visitors how much we really love them." He then began a countdown, "One…two…three." When he said *three*, the entire church jumped up in the air and shouted, "LEAP." The sound of hundreds of feet landing on the floor at the same time was something else!

Next, the pastor shouted "*L*," and the people shouted back, "Love everybody." He continued with an *E*, and they responded, "Evangelize everybody." Next came *A*, "appreciate everybody"; *P*, "pray for everybody." Then the audience began to clap and enthusiastically greet each guest.

Man, it was great! They flocked to me to shake hands, give hugs, pats on the back, and speak words of greeting. I will never forget it—especially the loud boom when all those feet hit the floor at the same time! I would not necessarily recommend duplicating this greeter scenario to everyone, but this pastor and people pulled it off beautifully!

• At the same church that gave the LEAP welcome, the pastor invited all visitors to meet briefly with him after the service in a specified room. Of course, I accepted the invitation. In addition to chitchat and light refreshments, the pastor explained in great sincerity a commitment he had made to God long ago.

He never wanted to preach a sermon that might leave questions in the minds of the hearers about God's plan of salvation. Although he had delivered a clear presentation of the gospel in his message that morning, at this time, he reiterated "how to be saved" and asked those present if there was anything that needed to be clarified for them. He told us that when he went into the ministry, he had promised

God he would make sure no one would ever leave his church service without hearing a clear presentation of the salvation message. From my perspective, the pastor's sermon was outstanding, and I appreciated his effort to take this extra step to make absolutely certain no one went away without knowing how to have a personal relationship with God through Jesus Christ. Man, we could use more like him!

• I thought it was a nice gesture when another church invited all the guests to attend a get-acquainted time after the service so "we can get to know you better." I made my way to the specified room and found it set with tables and chairs. Lemonade and an assortment of snacks were available self-service style. A number of folks had arrived before me, and others continued to come in.

It became apparent that all attendees were participating in this "let's get acquainted with our visitors" gathering. After selecting a few munchies, I carried on in my usual secret-church-shopper mode, sitting at an empty table right in the middle of the chatty crowd and waiting for someone to "get to know me." My wait turned out to be in vain. After a more-than-reasonable length of time, I trashed my paper goods and walked to my car—not one person ever spoke to me! What happened?[2]

THE BIBLE

It was interesting to see how Bibles were used in the various churches I visited. In this case, I am referring to the Bible as a book, not the message it contains.

I can remember a time when preachers would announce their sermon text and then comment on the "sweet sound of pages rustling" as the congregation turned the pages of their Bibles

---

2   The members seemed to enjoy socializing among themselves immensely! Seriously, I think someone had a good idea and good intentions, but the follow-through to train the people fell flat!

to the designated passage. Today it's more like the *sweet glow of smartphones* as people locate the text in their eBibles. I heard one pastor remark that he was rather disturbed to see so many people texting while he was preaching until it dawned on him they were more likely referring to their digital Bibles or taking notes on their smartphones. The Bible is the Bible regardless of the physical form it takes! I thank God for technology that makes the Word of God more accessible than ever before!

Here are some observations of how Bibles are used in worship services:

- Scriptures are printed in the bulletin or passages are displayed on a screen.
- The congregation is asked to stand as a sign of respect as the Bible is being read aloud.
- The congregation is asked to "take a Bible from the pew rack (or chair) and turn to page number ___."
- There are responsive readings, where the pastor alternately reads a verse and the audience reads the next.
- Attendees are asked to raise their hand if they did not bring a Bible. An usher would come forward with a loaner Bible. In some cases, the pastor invited guests to keep the Bible if they did not own one.
- The sermon text is displayed on the screens and read aloud in unison.
- Volunteers come forward to read the text from the pulpit.

Sad to say, in about 10 percent of the churches I visited, I never saw a Bible presented in any of the ways described above. The Bible and much of its message were completely absent. No wonder there was no apparent life in the service or the people!

I like this piece, which I took from a church bulletin:

> When you carry the Bible—Satan gets a headache.
> When you open the Bible—Satan collapses.

When you read the Bible—Satan loses his strength.
When you stand on the promises of the Bible—Satan loses
all power to harm you!

At the beginning of one church service I visited, attendees were asked to stand and hold their Bibles in the air (they all seemed to have one). Then they recited in unison the words that were colorfully and creatively projected on their screens (which most of them knew by memory). They called it *word up*. The pastor began with, "Let's word up":

> In the beginning was the *Word*
> The *Word* was with God
> The *Word* was God
> The *Word* is a lamp unto my feet
> And a light unto my path
> I will hide His *Word* in my heart
> That I might not sin against God
> Holy Spirit, give me ears to hear
> And strength to obey the *Word* of God!
> In Jesus's name—hallelujah!

What a way to begin every service! The intentional focus on the Word of God was evident in every aspect of the church!

One of many interesting features of the Messianic Jewish congregation I visited was their reverence for the Torah. The large decorative scroll was handled with great care and ceremony. The pastor and another person read from the scroll in much the same way as Jesus did on the Sabbath, as referenced in the book of Luke. A scroll does not lend itself well to skipping around from one passage to another like we can easily do with pages in a book. Therefore, the text of the scroll is read through from beginning to end, one predetermined segment each week until it is completed. Then it is rerolled and started over again.

Realizing this adds more impact to the account of Jesus (Luke 4:16–21) reading from the scroll in the Nazareth synagogue.

When He unrolled the scroll to the passage designated for that day's reading, it "just happened" to be a foretelling of Himself, to which He replied, "Today this scripture is fulfilled in your hearing." Amazing how God arranged that coincidence!

Well, back to the Messianic Jewish worship service I visited. After the day's reading from the Torah was completed, the scroll was rolled up then held upright in the arms of the pastor. Followed by a long line of men who had participated in the service from the platform, the Torah was paraded throughout the worship center, up and down the aisles and circling throughout. The worshipers gathered to the ends of the rows to line the aisles. As the Torah passed by, they touched their fingertips to their lips and then reached out to touch the scroll, symbolizing their love and devotion to the words it contained. Joyful, upbeat music, singing, and clapping accompanied the procession. It was a happy weekly routine that was fresh and celebratory in every way, with everyone in the room actively participating.

This was one of the most moving experiences of my entire church-visiting project! If only we all shared that exuberance for the Word of God, who knows how we could impact the world!

Whatever the case—use the Bible! May there be no mistaking where our foundational truths come from!

CORPORATE PRAYER

It did not take too many church visits for me to notice there is a general lack of prayer in worship services.

Many church services I visited included only a very brief prayer that seemed more like a formality than a genuine conversation with a loving Father. Often, prayers were read from a printed program, feeling perfunctory rather than heartfelt.

For decades, the typical times for prayer have been at the beginning and end of a service, with the traditional pastoral prayer somewhere in between. In today's highly programmed services, this format has often been altered. This is not necessarily a bad thing, depending on what is done instead.

As a former staff person, I am very familiar with the "we must stay on time" mentality and the legitimate reasons behind it. When there are multiple services on Sunday morning and the service runs over—chaos takes place, especially in the parking lots and in the children's ministries! I am well aware of the need to end on time.

Then there are so many worthwhile features to be included in the program lineup; it is difficult to know what to eliminate in the interest of time. Things to be considered are announcements, baptism, and special-emphasis days such as missions, Sanctity of Life Day, holiday programs, children's choir programs, high school and college graduation day, and youth camp reflections, to name a few.

Somewhere along the chain of command, decisions have to be made to determine what makes it on the schedule and how much time to allot for each. It's a tough issue to tackle! I'm afraid prayer is frequently cut altogether or drastically limited to make room for other things, and we are paying a high price for the omission!

I sincerely believe churches as a whole have lost their focus on corporate prayer. Rather than being removed deliberately, it has more likely happened gradually of seeming necessity without realizing the seriousness. Churches have simply become so organized they have become paralyzed trying to make everything fit. We must recognize prayer as the powerful lifeline of the church and restore its rightful place in our corporate worship!

We must realize as local church bodies and as individual believers that before God can do a work *in* us, He must do a work *to* us, which will allow Him to do a work *through* us. The vehicle for making this happen is prayer, both individually and collectively.

Here are some of the most powerful and effective examples of prayer that I have seen in worship services:

- A significant number of churches offer a time when attenders are invited to come forward to kneel or stand at the altar to pray. A time of silent prayer may be allowed, often with soft instrumental, musical accompaniment, concluding with an audible prayer by the pastor or another church leader. Many people generally respond and participate. A variation of this is when some churches invite folks to come to the altar to pray during the time of the come-forward invitation at the end of the service.

- Another practice common to quite a few churches is to invite folks with particular needs to come forward to have someone pray for them. Stationed all across the front of the auditorium are various couples or individual church members, as well as a few pastors, to serve as prayer partners. In every case where I have seen this done, the response is huge! Those waiting to be prayed for are usually waiting in line two to six persons deep. This apparently ministers to a great need among the people.

- This one is the most impactful of all. I saw a small number of pastors take a knee beside their pulpits and pour out their hearts to God. These were deeply moving expressions of praise, cries of repentance, and petitions for the spiritual needs of their church, community, and nation—sometimes accompanied by tears. What a great example this was to everyone! These pastors were wordlessly shouting by example, *Prayer is important in my church!*

I actually timed several of these pastoral prayers and found they ranged from two to eight minutes in length. That's a substantial amount of prayer time for a worship service. I found my thoughts alternating between *mental atta-boys* and *you better hurry up—you have a schedule to make.* Oops, how stupid of me! That's the old programmed pastor side breaking through! The "way to go" ultimately won out in my brain!

In all seriousness, I know of no more powerful way to develop the prayer life of a congregation than by the lead pastor's example of corporate prayer.

I have served as pastor of prayer in three different churches. Leading people to pray is by far the most difficult ministry I ever encountered. I have established intercessory-prayer ministries, taught classes on prayer, led prayer meetings, organized focused prayer campaigns, and published prayer guides. I believe all those are good things to do.

But I am convinced that the most effective way to actually get people to pray is through the example of their senior pastor, and the worship service is the place to do it. He might preach on prayer, and that is good. But by regularly listening in on the pastor's conversations with God, they learn how to pray and are motivated to pray. I firmly believe it is "caught," not taught. Think about it— how do children learn to pray? They mimic their parents' prayers.

A prerequisite for the pastor is that he have an active personal prayer life himself. His walk with the Savior must be pure and consistent—a fake will not cut it here.

Jesus's disciples were motivated by His relationship to the Father in prayer and asked Him to teach them to pray. He gave a model prayer for them to follow in formulating their own prayers.

Pastors, the ball is in your court! Our churches desperately need your example!

CHILDREN'S SERMON/CHILDREN'S CHURCH/ CHILDCARE

I have heard a lot of children's sermons during the months of my project. I have always enjoyed watching the faces of children as they listen to a message designed just for them. While the presenter speaks, most of the time, his entire congregation of little bodies seems to be enthralled. I "preached" many children's sermons over my fifty years in the ministry. One of my goals was to always let them know that they are loved and precious in Jesus's sight—always!

I remember one particular Easter Sunday morning when I was delivering a well-prepared and eloquent-in-my-eyes children's sermon. I figured I was doing pretty well because no one had a bad case of the "wiggles" yet. As usual, I was sitting on the steps leading to the stage area and was near the end of my spiel when a little boy stood up, climbed the steps toward me, got right in my face, and said, "You know what?" I just knew he was going to make a profound statement indicating the impact of my message, or perhaps he was going to say something complimentary about how wonderful my four-minute sermon was. I responded, "What?" He said, "My dog ate my sister's pencil," and he walked back to his place and sat down. Deservedly, my ego was sufficiently deflated!

Because children are so precious, a church needs to treat them in a very, very special way. There are varying schools of thought about what to do with children during the worship service. One view is to provide an age-appropriate children's church while parents are in "big church." This may or may not include a youth service for teenagers. Another view is for kids to attend the regular worship service along with their parents. Personally, I do not see either view as right or wrong, good or bad, helpful or harmful. There are many different scenarios to consider to determine what is best for a particular congregation. Here are some considerations that favor children's church:

- Many children attend church without parents to sit with. Children's church can minister to them and, hopefully, in time, reach their parents too.
- Bible lessons are geared for their age level of learning and application.
- Parents have a chance to focus on the sermon without the distraction and discipline issues of children with them.

Here are some considerations that favor no children's church:

- Children learn to behave in the worship service.
- Children become accustomed to the adult worship service early in life and avoid a "transition" when they are older.

- Families benefit from the shared worship experience instead of all going their separate ways at church.

Not surprisingly, large churches are more likely to offer children's church and a youth service (larger facilities, more volunteers). Except for perhaps infant and preschool care, smaller churches generally do not have children's church or a youth service.

Although my church visits did not include visiting any children's church per se, I was made somewhat aware of what was going on in that area through comments made in the adult service and info printed in the bulletin. I also happen to know that the children's and youth services in most megachurches rival the experience in the main worship center in technology, drama, praise bands, and innovative and entertaining formats. In fact, they can be full-fledged theatrical extravaganzas every week. I sometimes wonder if it is conditioning those children to unrealistic expectations and might prove to backfire down the line.

Children's church basically fell into two categories:

1. Children are dropped off by parents in the children's church area upon arrival. Mom and Dad attend "big church" and pick up kids after their service is over.
2. Children attend the first part of "big church." A children's sermon is given, after which the kids are dismissed to children's church and picked up by parents later.

One of the best children's sermons I heard was delivered by a young and excited pastor. He taught a great object lesson, and the adults were listening as intently as the children. He then announced that it was now time for the kids to go to their children's church. As the kids were filing out, he announced to the audience, "If you are a guest and do not feel comfortable with your children in our nursery or children's church, we certainly understand, and they are welcome to stay here. However, if your baby gets fussy, we ask you to take them down this aisle"—he was pointing—"to our cry room.

That will make everyone happier. You may want to refer to your bulletin for more information about our children's church." Here is what was printed in their bulletin:

KIDS IN THE WORSHIP SERVICE

This worship service is designed for ages 6th grade and up. If you have a child below that age, we would ask that you take them out and check them in to our Kids Ministry. They will have a lot more fun, learn a key spiritual concept they will be able to remember and use and you will be able to fully enjoy this service. Our Kids Ministry is secure, safe, and every volunteer has had a thorough background check. The Kids Ministry staff is ready to check you in!

A couple of churches I visited had no childcare or children's church at all on Sunday mornings. One was extremely small, but the other was a bit more than average size. They called themselves a family church. The following explanation was printed in the bulletin of the larger church:

THE _____ CHURCH DIFFERENCE

You may be used to showing up at the front door of the church and having each member of your family ushered off to a different part of the campus for "age-appropriate" teaching. At our church, families stay together.

CHILDREN ARE WELCOME

Another thing you may find unique about our church is the inclusion of children in our worship service. Don't bother looking for the nursery; we don't have one. We encourage all families to bring their children into the sanctuary. Cooing babies don't bother us one bit. Moreover, we believe it is important for children to worship with their parents, and to be taught how to sit through the service. If your children are practicing their sin nature, you are welcome to remove them from the room and practice discipline.

Being in this church was a fun, uplifting, and enjoyable experience. I had thoughts that the all-ages-of-kids syndrome might be a problem, but it was not. There were a few baby sounds and a minimal number of potty breaks. Neither presented much of a distraction. After every Sunday morning service, the church has a "fellowship meal." Their bulletin reads:

FELLOWSHIP MEAL

After the service, we invite you to join us for a fellowship meal. The families of our church have brought food that we would love to share with you. We think worship is about more than just music and preaching. Fellowship is a lost art we'd like to help you rediscover.

As soon as their worship service was over, I watched the transformation of their sanctuary into a dining hall. The men and boys started moving chairs and setting up tables. The ladies headed for the kitchen. The teenage boys began to bring out crushed ice, cups, and lemonade and began to fill the cups with ice. The teenage girls began to place napkins, salt and pepper, etc., on the tables. (I didn't just stand there—I helped move two chairs!) This statement is printed at the top of the bulletin, "Our Church Only Works If You Work It."

Unfortunately, some of my experiences with children's church or children's sermons were quite disappointing. Several churches listed children's sermon in their bulletins, and when it was announced, no children came forward. Other churches had only one or two children. This was a sad thing to me. I know for a fact that children's church and children's sermons have been used by our Lord to plant the seed of salvation or a call to missions in the hearts of many children.

I also heard children's sermons that were way too boring and dull, presented by a person who was way too boring and dull. The best children's sermons I've heard are well prepared and prayed over by an enthusiastic presenter, using a prop to make a Jesus-centered point in a brief amount of time.[3]

Here's a shocker for you! I attended a very large church and was surprised by the number of small children in the lobby area. As I "lingered" (as was my custom) in the foyer, I thought to myself that the service that morning was probably a special family service or a kids' day. I entered the large auditorium and found a seat. It was filling up quickly, and there were lots of kids everywhere.

A young dad with three small children came to my pew and sat down beside me. He was the first person to speak to me so far all morning, and he explained that his wife was sick at home and he had the children by himself that day. The service began—a very formal and traditional service. The three kids beside me (probably about ages seven, five, and four years) were acting just like restless kids, which was fine with me. Twice the dad apologized to me for their wiggles and restlessness.

As the service progressed, it was obvious that this was not a special kids' service. As I was reading their lengthy bulletin, I read these exact words: "Childcare: $4 cash per child due at drop-off." What? The man beside me would have to pay $12 a week, $48 a month, and $576 a year to put his three children in the nursery. No wonder there were so many kids in the worship center! I was blown away!

---

3   Some of the children's sermons I heard were much better than the big-church sermons!

4

Let's Visit a Church Together
The Service Continues

As the worship service progresses, we reach what would be considered by most to be the high point—the sermon. However, we must recognize that every element is significant in the overall worship experience. Here are the areas of focus at this time:

- Baptism
- Lord's Supper
- Sermon
- Invitation
- Announcements
- Offering

BAPTISM

Out of the many churches I visited, I witnessed baptism in only nine of them. Although baptism is not necessarily a weekly occurrence in any given church, I was a little surprised that I did not encounter more. I was encouraged to see several announcements in bulletins about upcoming baptism services and preparation classes. Some churches baptize monthly with the entire service built around it, but more often, they baptize "as needed."

One church baptized sixteen people and invited all of them and their extended family members to a celebration lunch immediately after the service. With only a couple of exceptions, most of the baptisms I witnessed were by immersion. I discovered that even some denominations that historically have favored sprinkling are now immersing instead.

In addition to the longtime, customary baptistery built in a highly visible spot in the front of the worship center (often projected on screens), I saw the following alternatives:

- A lovely outdoor baptistery is constructed in a beautifully landscaped courtyard adjacent to the worship facility. Church members gather around after the worship service to witness the baptisms. I suspect they schedule baptisms only during the warm-weather months.
- A large portable baptistery is moved into the worship center as needed. I'm a city boy, but I could best describe this as resembling a galvanized horse trough—seen in more than one church—both rectangular and round shapes.
- At a cowboy church, a *real* horse trough serves as a baptistery. Another alternative they employ—the bed of a large pickup is lined with heavy plastic, filled with water, and accessed via stepladder.
- A beach-community church I visited holds their regular worship service on the beach once a month in order to baptize in the surf. It always draws a crowd and has proven to be an effective outreach to outsiders.
- A residential swimming pool is used for baptism, which occurs during the week with a video shown in the Sunday morning service.
- Public swimming pools, hotel pools, and large inflatable backyard pools are also utilized by home churches or others with no official baptistery.
- Churches without their own baptistery may opt to "borrow" another church's facility for a baptismal service.

Officiating pastors and/or baptismal candidates have been seen dressed in white robes, special printed-for-the-occasion T-shirts, or casual street clothes such as jeans or shorts.

With the practicality of multiuse spaces in today's newer church facilities, the above are innovative options to meet the need for sufficient water to immerse without the permanency of a built-in baptistery. It is the symbolism of baptism that is important—the death, burial, and resurrection of Jesus, picturing our new life of identifying with Him. Whether in rivers, creeks, ponds, or oceans, biblical accounts of baptism, as well as other historical baptismal practices, utilized whatever water source was readily available to immerse individuals.

The success of a church is not measured by the attendance, facilities, music ministry, or the size of the benevolence budget. The spiritual thermometer of a church is how many people are being saved. Baptism is the visual public testimony of the person's new birth and commitment to follow Christ. When a lot of people are being baptized, that is evidence that the gospel is being preached, members are sharing their faith with others, Jesus is the priority and focus, and the Holy Spirit is moving in the church. When this happens, all ministries will be much healthier.

LORD'S SUPPER

The Lord's Supper is a very special way to remember the sacrifice of Jesus in our behalf and to worship Him for His great love. There is the potential for this ordinance to become boringly ritualistic and meaningless. May it never be!

My 100+ church visits exposed me to a wide variety of methods to employ when observing the Lord's Supper. In most churches, open communion was offered; meaning, it was open for any Christ follower to participate without being a member of that particular local church. However, I also attended some churches that announced their Lord's Supper service was "closed" to nonmembers.

There are many ways to conduct and serve the Lord's Supper. Basically, the elements are either distributed to the participants in some way, or the participants come forward to the altar to be served. I encountered far too many variations of this format to warrant a detailed explanation of each. Since I made one visit to each church, it was difficult to know the frequency that the Lord's Supper was served. For many, I got the impression that it was a weekly occurrence.

The elements used for the Lord's Supper are the following:

- Grape juice, wine, or a choice of the two (one church served water)
- Commercial wafer specifically made for this use
- Crackers (unleavened, whole or broken in pieces)
- White bread, wheat bread, other types of bread (pieces to be torn off whole loaf or already in pieces)
- Gluten-free bread (available in a few churches)
- Prepackaged-wafer-and-juice combo

My Worst Experiences with the Lord's Supper

Upon entering the worship center, everyone was handed a prepackaged Lord's Supper juice cup with a tiny wafer. While the offering was being taken, the attendees were instructed to "take the elements at this time." There was no prayer, no scripture, no explanation, no nothing. To me, it was a cold and meaningless experience!

In fact, there were several churches that served the Lord's Supper without saying a word about it. They merely passed around the elements with no reference to the significance and no biblical teaching.

I can't judge the hearts and minds of each individual participant. It is within the realm of possibility that they experienced a quiet moment of worship as they gratefully reflected on the sacrifice of Jesus in that brief moment. However, it seems to me that communion offered in this offhand manner week after week could easily become a mere formality with little or no thought about what it represents. If I were a nonchurched visitor, I would have no idea what was going on.

Even for those of us who know about the symbolic meaning of the juice and bread, representing the shed blood and broken body of Jesus and His admonition to "do this in remembrance of Me," the observance is greatly enhanced when presented along with some measure of scriptural teaching.

My Best Experiences with the Lord's Supper

The pastor gave a minisermon concerning the Lord's Supper then led the church in an extended pastoral prayer (five to seven minutes). Next, he instructed the people to be sure to "get right with God" and then proceed to any table and partake. I counted more than twenty round tables positioned around the worship center (one of those multiuse spaces). He encouraged dads to serve their families, others to team up and serve one another, and make it a special time of prayer, praise, and commitment. He invited anyone who did not know Christ as their personal Savior to come to the front to deal with that issue first.

There were thirty-two prayer partners at the front of the church to receive people and pray with them. It was a crowded but meaningful scene. Observing the Lord's Supper took about twenty-five minutes, and it was quite a touching and special service. Seeing dads serving their families and praying together was especially exciting to me. My assumption is that this observance occurred periodically and not necessarily every Sunday.

Another church concluded the service with communion every week. Volunteers of a sufficient number to serve the large audience in a reasonable time stood across the front of the auditorium. Half were holding a round loaf of bread in a cloth napkin. Standing alternately with the bread people, the other half held a goblet filled with grape juice or wine (a verbal distinction was made to the crowd to identify which was which).

Everyone who cared to participate filed by the volunteers to partake. The one holding the bread looked into the eyes of the participant (as the participant tore off a piece of bread) and spoke these words: "This is My body which was broken for you." In a similar manner, the next volunteer made direct eye contact with the participant (as the morsel of bread was dipped into the liquid of their choice) with these words: "This is My blood which was shed for You." The impact was stunning—I felt like Jesus had just spoken directly to me, and I was moved to tears. That says it all! I can't remember a more meaningful communion experience.

SERMON

During my church visits, I was totally shocked—no, a better word would be *appalled*—by the lack of solid, biblically based, well-delivered sermons. In several instances, I would not have known I was in a church if I had not seen the name on the building. These "talks" may have been suitable for a Civic Club meeting, a self-help group, or a speech class presentation, but they seemed completely out of place in a church worship service. Early on in my church-visiting project, I often thought, where are the sermons that do the following:

- Exalt and magnify Jesus Christ?
- Are based on God's Word, the Bible, rather than cute little stories and personal opinions?
- Contain a clear, Bible-based explanation of how to receive salvation through faith in Jesus Christ?
- Extend an opportunity for individuals to accept Christ as their personal Lord and Savior while encouraging them to take that all-important step?

Here are some sermon titles I found listed in bulletins:

- Group 1 sermon titles

  o "Character Builders"
  o "A New You in a New Year"
  o "Matters of Conscience"
  o "Leftovers"
  o "A Positive Path"
  o "The Human World"
  o "Finding Waldo"
  o "The Story of the Bells"
  o "A Place to Give"

- Group 2 sermon titles

  o "Victory in Jesus"
  o "What Does the Christian Life Look Like?"
  o "Built to Serve the Savior"
  o "Lord, Teach Us to Pray"
  o "The Door to Christ"
  o "Trusting the God That Guides"
  o "Jesus's Guide to Survival"
  o "Praising Our Lord...No Matter What!"
  o "Spiritual Fitness"
  o "The Love of God...It Is to Be Shared"

I realize that you can't judge a book by its cover, and you can't judge a sermon by its title either. However, I listened to all these sermons and found the first list of titles to be shallow, experience-oriented talks based on humanism, personal opinion, cultural trends, and worldly influences. And I'm all for catchy sermon titles to grab the attention of the hearers, but this was not the case here.

What I heard pastors say from the pulpits at times made me think, *What? Where did he get that?* or *Does this guy even own a*

Bible? Here are three extreme examples. I could list more, but these will amply illustrate what I am referencing:

- The pastor held up an offering envelope and said, "Someone in the audience has a bad hip, and someone else has high blood pressure. The envelope is your prescription for healing. It is pregnant with blessing for you. Give liberally, and God will heal and bless you." It wouldn't take a great deal of perception to figure out the content of other sermons that would be heard in this church!

- At the end of the service, a pastor stood in front of the pulpit and addressed the congregation with outstretched arms, "As a called and ordained servant of Christ and by His authority, I therefore forgive you of all your sins in the name of the Father, Son, and Holy Spirit." I can almost hear the gasps as you read these words!

- I was present in a mainstream denominational church and noticed two apparently Middle Eastern ladies in their traditional dress sitting near the front of the church. When the pastor introduced them as the speakers for the morning, I anticipated they would share their testimony of coming to Christ for salvation and denouncing the pagan religion of their heritage. The pastor said that, as Christians, we should love everyone as God does. I certainly agree with that. He then introduced the two women and said they would "share their story."

  As it turned out, the ladies were dedicated, practicing Muslims who had been invited to speak to the group about their high and holy Day of Ashura celebration. An outline was passed out to the congregation that included an introduction of the speakers, a "Muslim's Perspective to the Universe," "Roles of Muslim Prophets," and an explanation of the history and importance of the traditional dish called the Ashure dessert. They took about twenty-five minutes, and not one Christian reference was mentioned—and no wonder. They were not Christians; they were dedicated Muslims. After they sat down, the pastor thanked them for sharing. He mentioned that the guests had made Ashure dessert, and everyone was invited to sample a dish afterward.

What was this guy thinking? Every pastor of a Christian church is to *shepherd the flock* of God. This includes protecting them from harm and leading them to proper nourishment. Does a true shepherd bring wolves right into the midst of his ignorant and defenseless flock? Without a doubt, God loves those precious Muslim women and others like them as much as He loves you and me. Jesus died on the cross for them just like He did for you and me. We are to extend to them Christian love. But that does not include giving them an open door to spread their beliefs right within the four walls of our church! Should a pastor relinquish his once-a-week opportunity to share the Word of God and substitute pagan theology instead? I can only imagine what his own sermons are like!

On a more encouraging note, I heard many great Bible-based, God-honoring sermons that were not only inspiring and uplifting but were also challenging and convicting. They were delivered in an engaging manner that communicated well with the listeners. It was obvious that these pastors were well prepared, Spirit-led, and in touch with their congregation's needs. The fact that so many of these dynamic preachers are young was a special thrill to me—the future of Christianity seems brighter because of them. I love seeing young guys passionate for Jesus and His church, so this was always a special delight to me!

Sermon-delivery styles vary a good bit and generally coordinate with the style of the overall church program. Some pastors still preach wearing a suit and tie, and clerical robes are common in certain denominations. The trend is toward more casual dress—everything from sport coat with no tie, casual slacks with a nice open-collar shirt or knit golf-style shirt, to jeans with T-shirt or other type of shirt. Shirts were worn both tucked or untucked. Five churches I visited had female head pastors—all five delivered their sermons wearing official clerical robes.

In a few churches that had multiple Sunday morning services of more than one music style, the pastor changed clothes to dress more in keeping with each. In a few churches, shorts and flip-flops worn by attenders was the norm—but I never saw a pastor dressed in that degree of casual.

As to preaching methods, the tried and true "pick a Bible text and expound upon it" format is still alive and well. The effectiveness of verse-by-verse scripture exposition transcends many generations and trends. May it ever be so!

However, I witnessed a vast array of innovative presentations that were masterfully used to nail home a point. I suppose the variety of sermon enhancements is limited only by the creativity of the pastor and perhaps his media team and/or worship leader. Today's technology lends itself well to engage all the senses and deepen learning of spiritual truths. Other elements of stage displays and arrangements add variety. Here are a few ideas I encountered (the list could be endless):

- Short videos are used to introduce a topic or illustrate a point—commercially produced for church use or produced in-house by the church media team. Also, video clips from TV shows, movies, sports, or news reports are employed to pique interest or add current relevance. Current events always work well.

- Special three-dimensional backdrops are constructed to create visual interest for a single sermon or throughout a series of messages.

- The pastor interviews several individuals while casually seated around a living-room-style furniture arrangement.

- The stage is set with various props. One example is a stage set with bow and arrows with a target and other archery illustrations. The pastor shot three arrows into the target to introduce the topic of "Missing the Mark." He was a pretty good shot, making it especially impressive!

- Pastors preach from iPads and eBibles, which is common, rather than from handwritten or typewritten notes stuck within the pages of a Bible.
- PowerPoint presentations with fill-in-the-blanks bulletin inserts are in the majority.
- Pastors sometimes deliver their message while seated at a barstool with a high table. The intent is most likely to come across as talking heart-to-heart with the listeners rather than appearing "preachy" behind a pulpit. They may sit awhile, stand awhile, and/or stroll around the stage a bit. One pastor even kept his coffee mug on the table to sip occasionally during his sermon.

One of My Favorite Innovative Message Deliveries

The evidence of this presentation's effectiveness is its clarity in my memory today. I was present for the first in a series of sermons titled "Mythbusters" at a particular church about midway into my church-visiting project. The stage was appropriately decorated with images to suggest movies or a movie theater. The bulletin insert listed various quotes from classic movies. Images of well-known movie DVD covers were displayed on the screens one by one. The idea was to match the quotes to the correct movie. I thought I was doing pretty well.

The quotes were things like, "Play it again, Sam," "Go ahead, make my day," and "If you build it, they'll come." Then came the zinger—none of the quotes were accurate. They were only similar to the actual words spoken in the movies. The sermon began with the statement (printed on the bulletin insert), "Sometimes when we get certain quotes and sayings from the Bible wrong, it's not just cute or funny—it has consequences!" This was the springboard from which the series was launched. Part I was the myth, "God Doesn't Give You More Than You Can Handle." The pastor then had the full attention of the audience as he developed the lesson with verse after verse from the Bible to demonstrate his point. No one nodded off during that sermon! I gave him an A+![1]

A word of caution: along with advanced technology, the expanded capabilities of large churches, and the prevalence of hyped-up church programs comes a very real and present danger. It scares me to think that members, as well as outsiders, may now evaluate a church and its ministries based on its sensory and emotional appeal. We live in an era saturated with over-the-top, high-impact, fast-paced, sensory-overloaded experiences through TV, movies, the Internet, DVDs, and more.

It is prudent for the church to try to keep pace to capture the attention of our "consumers," but we deal with a fine line here. Are we creating exciting, audience-pleasing, nonstop, highly entertaining programs to the point that a straight-from-the-Bible message preached from the pulpit by a faithful pastor seems dull? Is the bottom line feeding the sheep or entertaining the goats? This is an issue well worth pondering! If the strongest aspect of the service is not human hearts being penetrated by the Word of God and resulting in life-giving change, we're in trouble! The supernatural trumps the spectacular any day! We must find the point of balance—let's be very careful and prayerful about this.

---

1   There was a trend a while back to use brief live dramas as a tool to introduce or enhance a sermon message. I recall these as being sometimes quite effective, sometimes good in and of themselves, but not particularly relevant to the sermon message and, sometimes, a distraction due to poor-quality presentation. The drama trend seems to have faded into the sunset—I never witnessed a live drama in any church I visited. Just FYI.

INVITATION

When I use the word *invitation*, I am referring to a designated time in a worship service when a pastor "invites" individuals to respond to the gospel message. This is usually near the end of the service, and people are invited to do the following:

1. Accept Christ as their Lord and Savior
2. Rededicate their life to the Lord
3. Join the church
4. Give their lives to the full-time ministry
5. Come to the altar to pray

Let's take a closer look at each offered "invitation."

Accepting Christ

In order to extend an invitation, the pastor must have explained the how-to of accepting Christ for salvation. The invitation is designed to encourage and motivate a person to make this life-changing decision at this time. When a person does accept Christ, they are referred to as *born again* or *saved*.

During this invitation, the pastor is generally at the front of the church, urging people to respond by coming forward to make the greatest decision they will ever make. Dr. Billy Graham and other evangelists have effectively used this style of invitation for years. It was in this manner that I personally accepted Christ at a Billy Graham Crusade held in Houston's Rice University football stadium. Some churches provide other invitation options:

a. One comes forward and goes to another room for individual counseling.
b. One proceeds to a designated room at the conclusion of the service for individual counseling (without coming forward).
c. One fills out and returns a card indicating the decision (someone will make contact with them at a later time).

d. One signs up for a special class to learn more about being saved.

e. The pastor asks for a show of hands indicating a desire to receive salvation. He then may lead them to repeat after him a sinner's prayer or direct them to a counseling area.

f. Other similar options.

There are many acceptable modes of dealing with bringing people to faith in Christ. There is no specific right or wrong about it. Different people may respond better to one method than another. A variation or combination of the above may be used. Each individual pastor/church must decide what works best for them.

The most important things are (1) the pastor must clearly communicate how a person receives salvation as a gift of God's grace through faith in Jesus Christ, and (2) the pastor must offer an opportunity for a person to come to a point of decision. Every time an evangelistic sermon is preached, decisions are made. Some people decide, "I will accept Christ." Some decide, "I will not accept Christ." And others decide, "I'll wait 'til another day to make up my mind."

Would a salesperson ever make a sale if he presented his entire product spiel and didn't ask the customer to buy it? We're talking about salvation, a matter of eternal ramifications—we must make an effective "pitch" and attempt to close the sale!

A great tragedy I observed in visiting churches was that I heard many sermons that never mentioned anything at all about accepting Christ. I often heard about how to be a better person, live a moral life, be a success, and give to the church—but about how to be saved? Not so much.

The Bible refers to unsaved people as "dead." Dead people don't need to be instructed to do good things and live right—they need life! In John 10:10, we read that Jesus "came to give life and life more abundantly." It is a sad thing when a sermon is void of life's greatest offer and an invitation to receive it.

Out of one hundred churches I attended, *sixty-three* presented some type of invitation to accept Christ, and *thirty-seven* churches did not give an invitation of any kind.

Rededication

There are instances when an individual Christian may allow their relationship with the Lord to become cold and distant. Their walk with their Savior is not what it once was or should be, or perhaps they have fallen into sinful practices. The message of a particular sermon may convict them of their sin and cause them to desire a fresh start with God. The pastor may invite those who want to rededicate their lives to Christ to come forward to voice their situation to the pastor and be prayed for.

The pastor has nothing directly to do with the process of rededication. He delivers the message through which the Holy Spirit does the convicting. The pastor just ministers to the person. Rededication is between the person and God. Only a person who has previously accepted Christ as their personal Savior and Lord can rededicate their life. A nonbeliever cannot. Since Christ is not in their life, there is nothing to rededicate their life to.

Unfortunately, I heard very few churches offer an opportunity for folks to rededicate their lives. The "going forward" is not necessary. However, when a person publicly rededicates their life, it is an incredible testimony in front of their church family. Going public is an encouragement to the rededicated individual as others affirm them and commit to pray for them. And it demonstrates to all God's tremendous love and forgiveness for His children.

Join the Church

As a church visitor, I did not always know the policy regarding membership. When there was a come-forward invitation, folks were usually invited to join the church. In other cases, by way of visitor welcome, joining the church was mentioned, and those interested were asked to fill out a card found in the pew rack. Sometimes instructions for joining were printed in the bulletin. Other options included coming to a specified room after the service to discuss or attending a class to learn more about what it would involve. And in many cases, there was no mention at all of joining the church or church membership. In this latter scenario, it may or may not be an indication of no membership available.

The whole concept of church membership seems to be evolving. Millennials tend to shy away from joining anything. For this age-group, church membership is not important. And some of the older age-groups may not be joiners either. That view is likely due to the idea of commitment attached to membership, and younger folks today are reluctant to commit to anything. I know of some newer churches that carry no membership rolls whatsoever.

Traditionally, most evangelical churches have offered membership to any person who professes to have accepted Christ as their Savior. Some churches additionally require baptism by immersion for members. New-member classes, receptions, or dinners are sometimes offered along with membership.

Personally, I have seen dozens (more likely, hundreds) of people walk the aisle to join the church, never to be seen again. Church membership rolls are frequently packed with names of people who have joined and dropped out for unknown reasons or have presumably moved away with no trace of current contact information. The FBI probably couldn't find half of them! So what are we to do?

I strongly recommend an organized new-member follow-up plan that includes some type of new-member class or series of classes. A high percentage of people who participate in such a plan will be active members for years to come.

Another huge problem in today's churches is this—a high percentage of church members are not genuine born-again believers. Estimates by well-known figures such as Billy Graham and the Barna Group indicate 70 to 80 percent of church members across all denominations may not be truly saved. These members may think they are saved and may profess to be Christians; but their lifestyles, priorities, or attitudes would suggest otherwise. This is a staggering thought!

Upon a number of occasions, I have known of people enrolled in a new-member class who have realized their lostness and given their lives to Christ. Based on this and other factors, I strongly believe there is great value in offering a new-member class.

Advantages of Church Membership

1. It can anchor a person to a particular local church body, give a sense of belonging (*my* church), and foster a sense of commitment to service.
2. A membership roll provides vital contact information—for general communication and to prevent the dreaded falling-through-the-cracks possibility.

Advantages of New-Member Classes

1. Proven effective in retaining new members
2. Often a means of discipling new converts
3. Opportunity to nail down genuineness of salvation
4. Discover leadership qualities and enlist volunteers

Advantages of No Church Membership

1. The obvious—it's much simpler with no record-keeping.
2. The unchurched may feel freer to attend knowing there is no pressure (whether real or imagined) to join.

Surrender Your Life to Full-Time Ministry

Of all the church services I attended, I saw only one person come forward during an invitation to surrender their life to full-time ministry. It was a young man who knew the Lord was calling him to be a pastor. He was soon finishing college and had plans to enroll in seminary.

His decision to accept God's call to ministry had been contemplated over a period of many months, with much prayer on his part, as well as consultations with the pastor and other spiritual leaders. This Sunday morning service was the occasion he had chosen to make his decision public.

When this happens in a church, it is a very meaningful and inspiring event. The pastor introduced him and asked the church to commit to pray for him. About fifty to sixty people came forward to place a hand on him as a sign of spiritual support and unity while the pastor verbalized a prayer. Those who were unable to reach him joined in by placing their hands on the shoulders of other prayers as the group gathered in close.

There are many factors God uses to impress His call to ministry upon individuals, but a primary one is a pastor who emphasizes and communicates the need for full-time evangelists, pastors, preachers, and missionaries. A large number of people serving in a full-time capacity today came from highly evangelistic and mission-focused churches. A strong breeding ground for full-time ministers are strong churches.

Come to the Altar to Pray

In the churches where a come-forward invitation is given, the pastor may extend an opportunity for attenders to come kneel or stand to pray at the front of the worship center, as mentioned in the section titled "Corporate Prayer." Whenever I saw this appeal given, there were always some who participated. Sometimes the individual was joined by a volunteer who offered to pray with them, but most frequently, they were given this time for private prayer.

Other avenues for having someone pray for you include the following:

- Take a section of a bulletin tear-off or prayer request card in the pew rack to complete and return for a prayer team to pray for you.
- Come to a specified room after the service to request prayer.

ANNOUNCEMENTS

How many church announcements do you think I heard in sixteen months while visiting 115 churches? Lots! I suppose some are always necessary, but a church must be careful how they are presented and what amount of time they will require. Announcements can be a distraction and can disrupt the flow of the service. Some churches use their members to make announcements. In this case, the announcer should be coached to know exactly what to say, then stand up, speak up, shut up, and sit down.

When someone making the announcements pauses and says, "What room is this going to be in?" or "Where are they going to sign up?" or "What time does the nursery open?"—it just deflates the service. I know, I was sitting in *that* service. When I was pastoring, from time to time, I had volunteers make announcements using an interview format. I would hold the mic and ask questions. A word to the wise—the pastor always holds the mic!

A really nice way to present the Sunday morning announcements is by recording them and projecting them on the big screens. I have seen some outstanding attention-getting productions that make quite an impact. These videos have been shown just prior to the beginning of the service (perhaps continuously for five to ten minutes before) or during the service itself. Another option I observed is to play the video announcements while the offering plates are passed. This kills two separate time-eating birds with one stone!

There are two things I have always believed about making announcements in church:

1. The fewer, the better.
2. That is what bulletins, handouts, and brochures are for.

OFFERING

A lady walked into a Methodist church and asked to see a pastor about arranging a funeral. When the pastor appeared, he was compassionate, caring, and more than willing to help. The lady informed him that her favorite cat had died. The pastor replied, "I'm so sorry—we don't conduct funerals for pets." To which, she said, "Well, I *was* going to give a $15,000 gift to the church." He immediately responded, "Oh, I didn't know it was a Methodist cat." This gives us a chuckle, but it may be a realistic illustration of the urgency or even the desperation that many pastors feel to bring in the funds necessary to support the ministry of the church.

The topic of the offering, or the giving of material resources to the church to be used to finance its ministries, is often a touchy subject. Accusations of "all they talk about at that church is money!" are common. That is certainly an unfair exaggeration, but there is a bit of truth to it. Money is a necessity to operate a church, and God's people are to be the givers of what He has provided to them. Consequently, preachers must address the subject with a certain degree of regularity.

In every worship service I attended, an offering was collected in some way. The majority of pastors had something to say about the offering—from just a simple appeal to give; to a lengthy, emphatic, heart-wrenching plea; to a full-blown, hard-pressure, all-out, guilt-inducing sales pitch! A few churches had a printed reminder about the offering in the bulletin, and/or it was promoted on the big screens.

Here are some of the ways I saw offerings received:

- Offering plates are passed up and down the rows by ushers.
- Cloth bags with handles on each side are passed down the rows.
- An offering basket is placed on a table in front of the worship center—everyone passes by to drop in their offering.
- Large rectangular plastic stackable containers are distributed by ushers to each row to be passed down the row. They are collected at the opposite end by ushers and stacked one inside the other as they are collected. This is done quickly and efficiently.

- Stackable buckets preset under each aisle seat are passed down the row at the designated time and collected by ushers at the opposite end.
- At close of service, an announcement/reminder is given to have offerings ready to give. After a closing prayer, church officials stationed at exit doors collect offerings as attenders exit.
- No offering is collected during service. Offering boxes are attached to walls near entrances to the worship center for churchgoers to deposit offerings before and after service.
- Prior to offering collection, the pastor announces visitors are not expected to make a contribution. This serves to dispel the common notion of many unchurched people that "all they want is my money."

After the offering was collected, the ushers frequently placed it all on the table in the front, symbolizing giving it to the Lord, and prayer was offered to bless its use for ministry. In today's churches, this is an often overlooked means of depicting giving as an act of worship. Accompanied by a few appropriate comments, the practice can serve as a simple teaching tool to reinforce the biblical concept of giving.

Most, but not all, churches have printed offering envelopes available in pew racks. Often, offering envelopes are mailed to members on a monthly basis.

Church members are sometimes urged to sign pledge cards to fund the regular church budget or for special projects. The church may or may not follow up with invoices for the pledged amount. Other churches shy away from "forcing" a monetary commitment and shun the use of pledge cards altogether.

Many churches conduct some kind of fund-raising event from time to time for a special purpose but receive the vast majority of their funding from gifts and offerings. A few churches seem to be especially big on fund-raising projects such as bazaars, raffles, festivals, bingo, bake sales, craft shows, auctions, spaghetti suppers, garage sales, and any number of other endeavors.

To that, I would offer a word of caution: Most of these projects are quite labor-intensive, requiring much time and planning. Time and effort spent fund-raising is time taken away from ministry. Better stick to the basic biblical plan of *giving* by God's children.

Here are a couple of things I picked up on in my visits:

The good news. A growing number of churches, even large to megachurches, are becoming debt-free! I give them high fives and hallelujahs for that accomplishment! I can testify from my own experience of living debt-free on a personal level and being a member of a church that has been debt-free for over forty years—it is truly the way to go! I encourage and challenge every church to do the same. It *can* be done, and it will revolutionize your ministry! Go for it!

The bad news. Giving in churches, as well as giving to other nonprofits and parachurch ministries, is on the decline—in fact, it is at a critical stage. The majority of charitable giving comes from older people, and their numbers are naturally diminishing. Younger people are not prone to give like the generations before them. This is largely due to a general distrust that they feel about how the funds might be used or misused. And their fears are not without good reasons. Even within the church community, we read about financial scandals, see churches filing for bankruptcy, hear about building programs shut down because of insufficient funding, and know of churches refinancing loans. These sad stories go on and on. There is something terribly wrong with this picture! It is not surprising that our young people feel distrustful!

Another reason for the general lack of giving among younger people is that we have failed to adequately teach them the basic concepts of biblical giving. In an effort to be seeker friendly and nonoffensive, we have backed away from the topic of giving. Urging people to give without explaining God's principles of stewardship is doing them a disservice.

Giving is an act of love and worship. You cannot love someone or something and not support it in every way you can. I give to my church because I love Jesus. Here are some thoughts about giving:

1. Everything belongs to God—it is not my money or my stuff.
2. God expects us to be good stewards.
3. Our skills and abilities come from God.
4. Work is good and profitable.
5. We are to love God, not goods.
6. We are to be generous and compassionate.
7. We can never outgive God.

Show me your calendar and your checkbook, and I will show you where your heart is. Folks always spend their time and money on who and what they really love. If we all love God like we should, there would never be a need to appeal for funds. Giving is a natural part of loving God! See more on this topic in the chapter called "Are You Still Passing the Offering Plates?"

5

Let's Visit a Church Together
The Aftermath

The worship service may be over, but from the viewpoint of the visitor, they are still making judgments about the church and whether they will come again. The church's opportunity to reach out to every guest continues even after Sunday morning. Let's consider the following:

- Dismissal/exiting
- Church visitor follow-up
- Website
- Newspaper ads
- Multisite churches

DISMISSAL/EXITING

When exiting a church at the conclusion of the worship service, I usually had the same experience I had when I entered the building. If I was spoken to and warmly welcomed when I entered, I usually received the same treatment when the service was over. The "good morning" and "welcome" turned into "have a nice day" and "come back and see us." If I had been ignored upon arrival, the same held true for my departure.

Pastors often stand at the exit to speak to the people and give them an opportunity to have a one-on-one time with him, and that is a good personal touch. I've also seen the pastor mingling informally among the attenders in the lobby when the large numbers make it impossible to shake everyone's hand at the door. In other cases, the pastor is in another room where visitors have been invited to meet with him.

CHURCH VISITOR FOLLOW-UP

This is a most important ministry! Not contacting visitors is just like saying, "We don't care." I always look at it from this perspective: What if I were a hurting person looking for a look, word, and touch from the church and God? How would I feel about this church and about God? What if I were checking out different churches to select one to join? Would I feel like I would be accepted and fit in here? How can a church proclaim, "We love everybody," and never follow up by contacting a visitor? Any contact at all is better than none.

On the other hand, the nature of the contact received— promptness, sincerity, and warmth, individual attention versus form letter—can make all the difference in a visitor's desire to return. Here was my experience out of the selected one hundred churches I visited:

- 13 did not have visitor cards at all, leaving no doubt about their attitude toward guests.
- 87 had visitor cards, which I filled out and turned in. I checked yes to the question, "Do you want to be contacted?"
- 52 contacted me after my visit. The type and time of contact varied.
- 40 contacted me more than one time—kudos for this.
- 35 never contacted me in any way. It felt like a slap in the face.

Basically, the contacts received after a church visit fell into four categories: phone calls, letters, cards, personal visit. I intentionally eliminated the possibility of e-mail contacts by omitting my e-mail address on the visitor card. The other four options require a bit more effort than zipping off an e-mail—just wanted to check if that effort would be made.

I was on the receiving end of all four categories. The phone calls came from pastors or pastoral staff people, as well as volunteers, and most were cordial and friendly in nature.

Letters and cards ranged from mediocre and distant to informative and magnetic. A good many of the letters were way too long. For example, I received an 8-paragraph letter from a pastor that contained 537 words written in a 12-point font. It was obviously a form letter with a stamped signature run off on a copy machine. It had an impersonal feel and was much too wordy for the average person to read, making it rather ineffective for its purpose.

On the other hand, I received a brief twenty-one-word greeting, handwritten on a nice card, featuring the church logo and mission statement on the front. It was brief, to the point, and signed by the pastor. It read,

Dear Buddy,

Thank you for being our guest at _____ Church! We hope you come back soon.

All the best,
Senior Pastor

Very well done! I read every word of it!

Only in one instance was my church visit followed by a personal visit to my home. After the worship service, I ate lunch at a nearby restaurant then went home, changed clothes, and assumed my Sunday-afternoon-chill-out mode. Shortly thereafter, the doorbell rang; and I wondered, *Who in the world could that be?* My wife answered the door, and I quickly realized she was inviting someone into the house! Uh-oh—that was my cue to make a hasty exit since my chill-out attire was not suitable for entertaining guests!

After a mad dash to the bedroom to become more appropriately clad, I was introduced to a friendly and efficiently trained volunteer from the church where I had spent the morning. As we began a comfortable conversation, his preliminary remarks included questions that might be typically asked of a church prospect to help him discover my spiritual status in relation to God. I could not keep up the pretense any longer. I explained to him my secret-church-shopper mission, and we had a wonderful discussion about their church and its ministry. Man, was I impressed!

I confess to having the fleeting thought that someone might have tipped him off as to my project, and he was there so promptly to improve the score I would be giving for his church. I was wrong! I later learned from another pastor in that same suburban neighborhood that this church is known for their follow-up policy of making a same-day home visit to every Sunday morning first-time guest. And they have been consistently doing this for a number of years! Wow! That is remarkable! They have undoubtedly reaped the benefits!

Here's a visitor follow-up tactic I found to be unique and really cool! This does not exactly fall within any of the four usual categories mentioned above. On Tuesday, I received in the mail a package—with no return address except a small logo I did not initially recognize. The corrugated cardboard box contained a copy of the book *How Good Is Good Enough?* by Andy Stanley. There was nothing else in the box—no note, no letter, nothing. Hmmm, where did this come from?

The very next day, Wednesday, I received a phone call from a staff member of the church I had visited the previous Sunday. After identifying himself and making a few other opening remarks, he said, "Did you receive the book we sent you?" Curiosity satisfied! I was compelled to share with him my reason for visiting his church, and we had a great conversation. A few days later, I received a nicely done letter and Starbucks gift card from the same church. The entire church-visit experience had been excellent—everything was top-notch! It was not surprising that their outreach approach is appealing and apparently fruitful!

WEBSITE

An important step in planning for each of my church visits was to visit their web page. This gave me a preview of the overall church ministry as well as specific information I needed, such as general location, physical address, phone number, driving directions, and times of services. This means I tried to go to 115 websites. Although the vast majority of churches I visited have a website, some did not. Worst of all—some have inaccurate information! I could use the following terms in describing church websites:

- Simple
- Elaborate
- Easy to navigate
- Difficult to navigate
- Helpful
- Confusing
- Out-of-date information
- Accurate information
- Poor quality of design
- Grammatical and spelling errors

"People will visit a church web page before they visit your church." This statement, in one form or another, was shared with me by leaders of six different denominational associations whom I consulted with.

In today's computer-driven culture, a website for your church is a *must!* The Internet is the first source of information to be referenced on any topic. No longer is a web page considered a unique option or luxury—today it is a vital necessity! This will become increasingly true with every passing year.

Companies that deal with web design are everywhere. In fact, there is likely someone in each church knowledgeable in setup or maintenance of the site. Large churches hire full-time staffers to manage the website. In other situations, volunteers with the right computer savvy are utilized to provide this ministry.

The website is the digital face of the church. We must look our best. Whenever a person visits a church web page, they are demonstrating enough interest to "check it out." This is truly their first look at the church. Whatever they see there, they will project as the image of the actual church. Therefore, a church needs to give great attention to the design, maneuverability, and accuracy of the site to meet the needs of the inquirer.

If you have a website, whatever you do, keep it current! What does it say to the reader when they find events listed that happened two months ago? I repeat, if you don't have a website, get one! Websites used to be a unique option or a luxury—today they are a vital necessity!

NEWSPAPER ADS

Part of my secret-church-shopper routine was to read a Saturday section of the *Houston Chronicle* newspaper titled, "Worship Community." I began regularly viewing this three-quarter-page feature, hoping to keep tabs on what's going on in Houston-area churches.

Occasionally, announcements of special events such as conferences, outstanding guest speakers, concerts, revival meetings, and church anniversary celebrations have appeared. Other than that, the regular ads list the names of churches by denomination with their service times, addresses, phone numbers, web address, and pastor's name. For sixteen months, churches of the same five denominations have advertised in this section—one Anglican, one Assembly of God, two Baptist (one with six campuses and one with five campuses), one Roman Catholic, and two Methodist (one with two campuses).

Does advertising in a citywide newspaper help? Is the return worth the investment? Do people respond to the newspaper advertisements? I really don't know the answer to those questions.

The church advertisers mentioned represent only a small fraction of the total number of churches located in the huge metropolitan Houston area. I would be surprised if the info is greatly utilized.

I have been glad to see that the church family has some kind of presence in the newspaper, small though it may be. It was a refreshing reading reprieve mingled among the articles concerning crime, politics, social unrest, and other gut-wrenching happenings that seem to dominate our society.

MULTISITE CHURCHES

Many larger churches have satellite campuses scattered in strategic locations around the city and its suburbs in addition to their main campus. Since megachurches typically have members living in all parts of the city, they have a built-in volunteer base to help jump-start a new church. Generally, the mother church acquires a temporary facility to begin. Next, they round up a nucleus of their own existing members who live in the target area and who will commit to attend and/or provide leadership for the new church start.

A minimum commitment of twelve to twenty-four months is typically requested, and most responders wind up remaining at the new site. Usually an on-site home team is brought in, consisting of a lead pastor, worship leader, and praise band. This *live* team leads the worship portion of the service. Then as the senior pastor preaches from the main campus, his sermon is live-streamed to all the satellite locations, after which the home team closes out the service. All programs, ministries, activities, and special events of the main campus are duplicated at each satellite location, under the direction of the senior pastor and staff of the home church.

The beauty of this model can be seen in at least three ways: (1) The initial leadership group recruited to attend at the new location has the benefit of everything they experienced and liked at the main campus, including the preaching of the senior pastor—and they have it close to home! (2) An active, thriving, vibrant church hits the ground running, and is a big church from day one, ready to reach out to the new community—instant church! (3) Often, a permanent church building of sizeable proportions and capabilities is constructed very soon after the start-up. In fact, in some cases, the new church opens with a new building already constructed.

Currently in the Greater Houston area, the most satellite campuses one church operates is six, with plans to expand. A recent nationwide church survey reported that six thousand churches in America have multicampus services. As a whole, multisite churches have proven to be effective—I say, way to go!

There are a few possible repercussions to the multisite plan that could prove challenging for the mother church:

1. It may become overextended and have difficulty sustaining itself.
2. It may underestimate the added financial, personnel, pro-gramming, and maintenance obligations, as well as logisti-cal challenges.
3. If the founding senior pastor retires or moves on, finding a replacement with adequate leadership qualities and drive could be difficult.

Here's another challenge I have witnessed firsthand that is quite disturbing. There had been slow but steady growth in a particular community for years; and then with the construction of a brand-new state-of-the-art high school, a middle school, and two new elementary schools, there was an explosion of growth. A new freeway opened, businesses were popping up everywhere, and residential development was at a high. A megachurch came in to establish a satellite campus. They rented one of the brand-new elementary schools, publicized their opening day, brought in a talented praise team, set up a first-class worship center, and focused on establishing a dynamic youth ministry.

Their first-class mail outs flooded all residential areas, inviting everyone to the opening day. There would be free breakfast for all. Their knockout band and free breakfast would be an every-Sunday attraction. They were very successful! More than four hundred people attended on the first Sunday, including over one hundred youth. They were off to a great start!

So what was the problem? There was another smaller church located less than four hundred yards from the new elementary school that served as the megachurch's Sunday worship center. The smaller church had been slowly but surely growing during the six years of their existence. With a prior knowledge of the new schools to be built, they had put a lot of time, energy, personnel, and resources into building a strong youth ministry.

I visited with the pastor of the small church a couple of months after the megachurch began services. Many of their youth attended the first megachurch service and had never come back. The teenagers eventually invited their church friends, who did the same. The pastor told me that he had never been contacted by the megachurch and concluded by saying, "We simply can't compete with them." I checked back with the pastor a couple of months later and found that many of the parents had followed their kids, and the small church was really hurting because of it.

This difficult situation can be compared to the Wal-Mart scenario. Many small towns with thriving mom-and-pop businesses experience negative effects when a Wal-Mart moves into town. Wal-Mart offers long and convenient hours of operation, a huge variety of products, employment opportunities, and lower prices that the mom-and-pop stores cannot compete with. Many close after having been in business for years.

I was recently in a town that had experienced the Wal-Mart effect. Before Wal-Mart moved in, there were about thirty different stores and eateries operating around their town square. Wal-Mart opened on the interstate about half a mile from the center of town. The interstate has taken all the traffic, and Wal-Mart has taken all the customers. I drove around the square and counted only eleven stores still in operation, which means nineteen had closed.

What is the solution to the Wal-Mart effect in the church world? I hope someone has some answers—and they better be good ones!

Thanks for going to church with me! It was fun to be together and worship side by side.

Let me leave you with this profoundly deep and life-changing truth—"Jesus loves me, this I know, for the Bible tells me so." I pray that this is the message your church and every church is proclaiming.

See you next Sunday!

6

Lists, Facts, Figures, and Paper Tools

Here you will find lists of the churches I visited, as well as the statistical information gathered. Also included is some explanation of the process used to put it all together. It is important to keep in mind that my primary goal in doing this is to provide firsthand information for the church to advance the kingdom of God.

The chapter is divided into three sections:

1. Lists of churches

    *   Alphabetical
    *   Denominational

2. Facts and figures (Answers to these questions and more than fifty others are given.)

    *   How many churches had baptism as part of their service?
    *   Was I contacted after I visited?
    *   What types of worship services did I discover?

3. Paper tools

Learn about the forms I designed and discover the procedure used to gather accurate information and make comparisons.

When I first started visiting churches with the intent of evaluating each in an organized way to share with the pastor, I set a goal of fifty churches. After getting into it a bit, I realized that might not be enough, and I was eager to take it further. After prayer, much thought, and personal soul-searching, I settled on one hundred churches. It seemed like a good round number and makes the math easier in calculating percentages.

In time, I made a discovery. Some of the churches did not have what would be considered a typical Sunday morning service on the day I visited. I ran into various not-your-ordinary-service, special programs such as a children's choir music program, mission-trip report to the church, school graduation, Christmas concert, and others. It wouldn't quite be comparing apples to apples to include these visits in my stats on one hundred churches.

Another factor influenced the way the church visits were considered in my reporting. Because the doctrinal stance of some religious groups was not at all in keeping with biblical teachings, they were eliminated from the one hundred. To see for myself what is going on among these groups was informative, so I'm glad I went. Beyond that, I would violate my own stated purpose to deal with them further. Remember—my goal is to *advance the kingdom of God*. It would take much more than a secret-church-shopper report to set them on a path of advancing the kingdom of God!

According to the qualifications just given, 100 churches were selected from the 115 to be the basis of most statistics and comparisons. This is not to say that my experiences in the additional 15 churches have been ignored in this book. There are places where I have shared comments about things I saw and heard from the 15 extra visits. However, I sent letters and reports to only 100 churches, and I used the same 100 churches to compile my statistics.

I realize that to visit a church for only one Sunday is like reading only one chapter in a book with fifty-two chapters. The Sunday I attended could have been a really good day or more of an off day. It would be pretty difficult for me to know. But I believe that, in the long run, it all averages out and results in valid and useful info.

After I increased my desired number of church visits to one hundred, I began to double up each Sunday when possible. With a minimal amount of preplanning to attend two churches in close proximity, I was often able to make it to an early service at one and drive to another late-morning service close by.

All of my activity centered in the rapidly growing Greater Houston metroplex, located in the southeast coastal area of Texas with a population of more than eight million. Historically, the area has been considered to be a part of the Bible Belt, although that designation may no longer be deserved. The extremities of my visits reached as far north as Conroe, south to Galveston, west to Sealy, and east to Winnie.

As you might guess, reaching 115 church destinations required a good bit of driving and gasoline. The church closest to my home was less than a quarter of a mile, and the one farthest from my home was 116 miles, averaging 35.8 miles per round trip. For a grand total, I added 4,122 miles on my car—and one flat tire! Oh, happy day!

ALPHABETICAL LIST OF CHURCHES VISITED

The attempt was made to be accurate in listing the official name of each church. Occasionally the name varied slightly in printed literature. Any discrepancies in this list are unintended.

All are Houston addresses unless otherwise noted.

A
All Around Cowboy Church (Sealy)
Ashford Community Church
Ashford United Methodist Church

B
Bay Area First Baptist Church (La Marque)
Berachah Church
Bethel Church

Braeswood Church
BridgePoint Bible Church

C
Calvary Baptist Church (Rosenberg)
Champion Forest Baptist Church
ChangePointe Church (Conroe)
Chapelwood United Methodist Church
Christ Evangelical Presbyterian Church
Christ Memorial Lutheran Church
Christ the Servant Lutheran Church
Church at the Cross
Clay Road Baptist Church
Clearpoint Church
Coastal Community Church (Galveston)
Cokesbury United Methodist Church (Pasadena)
Community of Faith (Hockley)
Concordia Lutheran Church
Congregation Beth Israel
Congregation Beth Messiah
Cornerstone Church (Winnie)
Covenant Community Church (Pearland)
Covenant Presbyterian Church
Crosspoint Church (Bellaire)
Crosspoint Community Church (Katy)
Crossroads Fellowship
Current, A Christian Church (Katy)

E
Ecclesia
Emmanuel Episcopal Church

F

Faithbridge (Spring)
Faith Memorial Baptist Church
Family Life Assembly (Katy)
Fellowship of the Nations
First Baptist Church (Pasadena)
First Baptist Church (Pearland)
First Baptist Church of Katy (Katy)
First Colony Church of Christ (Sugar Land)
First Metropolitan Church
First Presbyterian Church
Freedom Fellowship (Pearland)

G

Gateway Community Church (Webster)
Grace Assembly (Braeswood, West Campus)
Grace Church (Humble)
Grace Community Church (Gulf Freeway)
Grace Community Church (Spring Branch)
Grace Family Baptist Church (Spring)
Grace Point Community Church
Grace Presbyterian Church
Greater Macedonia Baptist Church
Greenhouse Community Church

H

Harvest Christian Fellowship
Higher Dimension
Holy Rosary Catholic Church (Rosenberg)
Holy Spirit Episcopal Church
Hope Lutheran Church (Friendswood)
Houston International Seventh-Day Adventist Church
Houston's First Baptist Church

K

Kingsland Baptist Church (Katy)
Kirkwood South Christian Church

L

Lakewood Church
LifePointe Fellowship (Pearland)
Live Oaks Friends Meeting

M

McGee Chapel Missionary Baptist Church
Memorial Church of Christ
Memorial Drive Christian Church
Memorial Drive Presbyterian Church
Memorial Drive United Methodist Church
Memorial Lutheran Church

N

Neartown Church
Northeast Houston Baptist Church (Humble)
North Oaks Baptist Church (Spring)

P

Parkway Fellowship (Katy Campus)
Parkway Fellowship (Richmond Campus)
PowerHouse Church (Katy)

S

Salem Evangelical Lutheran Church
Second Baptist Church (Woodway Campus)
Servant-Savior Presbyterian Church
Servants of Christ United Methodist Parish
Seventh Church of Christ, Scientist
Sugar Land Baptist Church (Sugar Land)

St. Basil the Great Greek Orthodox Church
St. Charles Borromeo Catholic Church (Katy)
St. Christopher's Episcopal Church
St. Cyril of Alexandria Catholic Church
St. Edith Stein Catholic Church (Katy)
St. Matthew Lutheran Church
St. Paul's United Methodist Church
St. Peter's United Methodist Church (Katy)
St. Timothy's Anglican Church
St. Thomas Presbyterian Church

T
Tallowood Baptist Church
Texas Cowboy Church (Orchard)
The Ark Church (Conroe)
The Bridge (Sugar Land)
The Church at Bethel's Family
The Church of Jesus Christ of Latter Day Saints, Ashford
The Church Without Walls
The Encourager Church
The Foundry United Methodist Church
The Met
Trinity Episcopal Church

U
Unity of Houston

V
Vineyard Church of Houston

W
Westheimer Community Church
West Houston Seventh-Day Adventist Church
West Oaks Fellowship

Westside Church of Christ (Pearland)
Westside Church of the Nazarene (Katy)
Wheeler Avenue Baptist Church
Wilcrest Baptist Church
Woodlands Church (The Woodlands)

DENOMINATIONAL LIST
OF CHURCHES VISITED

There are twenty-eight denominations listed. When the church name does not include a denominational name, the pastor or another church representative was asked if the church was a denominational church or an independent church. They are categorized in this list accordingly. Any discrepancies are unintended.

1. Anglican (1)

    • St. Timothy's Anglican Church

2. Assembly of God (4)

    • Braeswood Church
    • Cornerstone Church (Winnie)
    • Family Life Assembly (Katy)
    • Grace Assembly (Braeswood, West Campus)

3. Baptist (30)

    • Bay Area First Baptist Church (La Marque)
    • Calvary Baptist Church (Rosenberg)
    • Champion Forest Baptist Church
    • Clay Road Baptist Church
    • Clearpoint Church
    • Coastal Community Church (Galveston)
    • Crosspoint Church (Bellaire)
    • Ecclesia
    • Faith Memorial Baptist Church
    • Houston's First Baptist Church

- First Baptist Church of Katy (Katy)
- First Baptist Church (Pearland)
- First Baptist Church (Pasadena)
- Greater Macedonia Baptist Church
- Kingsland Baptist Church (Katy)
- McGee Chapel Missionary Baptist Church
- Neartown Church
- Northeast Houston Baptist Church (Humble)
- North Oaks Baptist Church (Spring)
- Parkway Fellowship (Katy Campus)
- Parkway Fellowship (Richmond Campus)
- Second Baptist Church (Woodway Campus)
- Sugar Land Baptist Church (Sugar Land)
- Tallowood Baptist Church
- The Bridge (Sugar Land)
- The Church at Bethel's Family
- The Church Without Walls
- The Met
- Wheeler Avenue Baptist Church
- Wilcrest Baptist Church

4. Bible (1)

   - BridgePoint Bible Church

5. Catholic (4)

   - Holy Rosary Catholic Church (Rosenberg)
   - St. Charles Borromeo Catholic Church (Katy)
   - St. Cyril of Alexandria Catholic Church
   - St. Edith Stein Catholic Church (Katy)

6. Christian / Disciples of Christ (2)

   - Kirkwood South Christian Church
   - Memorial Drive Christian Church

7. Christian Missionary Alliance (1)

- Greenhouse Community Church

8. Church of Christ (3)

- Memorial Church of Christ
- First Colony Church of Christ (Sugar Land)
- Westside Church of Christ (Pearland)

9. Christian Scientist (1)

- Seventh Church of Christ, Scientist

10. Covenant (1)

- Covenant Community Church (Pearland)

11. Episcopal (4)

- Emmanuel Episcopal Church
- Holy Spirit Episcopal Church
- St. Christopher's Episcopal Church
- Trinity Episcopal Church

12. Foursquare (1)

- Current, A Christian Church (Katy)

13. Greek Orthodox (1)

- St. Basil the Great Greek Orthodox Church

14. Independent (22)

- Ashford Community Church
- Berachah Church
- Church at the Cross
- ChangePointe (Conroe)
- Crossroads Fellowship

- Community of Faith (Hockley)
- Fellowship of the Nations
- First Metropolitan Church
- Grace Community Church (Gulf Freeway)
- Grace Community Church (Spring Branch)
- Grace Church (Humble)
- Grace Point Community Church
- Harvest Christian Fellowship
- Higher Dimension
- Lakewood Church
- LifePointe Fellowship (Pearland)
- PowerHouse (Katy)
- Texas Cowboy Church (Orchard)
- The Ark Church (Conroe)
- The Encourager Church
- West Oaks Fellowship
- Woodlands Church (The Woodlands)

15. Jewish Messianic (1)

- Congregation Beth Messiah

16. Jewish Orthodox (1)

- Congregation Beth Israel

17. Lutheran (8)

- Christ the Servant Lutheran Church
- Christ Memorial Lutheran Church
- Concordia Lutheran Church
- Crosspoint Community Church (Katy)
- Hope Lutheran Church (Friendswood)
- Memorial Lutheran Church
- Salem Evangelical Lutheran Church
- St. Matthew Lutheran Church

18. Methodist (10)

- Ashford United Methodist Church
- Chapelwood United Methodist Church
- Cokesbury United Methodist Church (Pasadena)
- Faithbridge (Spring)
- Gateway Community Church (Webster)
- Memorial Drive United Methodist Church
- Servants of Christ United Methodist Parish
- St. Peter's United Methodist Church (Katy)
- St. Paul's United Methodist Church
- The Foundry United Methodist Church

19. Mormon-LDS (1)

- The Church of Jesus Christ of Latter Day Saints, Ashford

20. Nazarene (1)

- Westside Church of the Nazarene (Katy)

21. Pentecostal (2)

- All Around Cowboy Church (Sealy)
- Freedom Fellowship (Pearland)

22. Presbyterian (8)

- Bethel Church
- Christ Evangelical Presbyterian Church
- Covenant Presbyterian Church
- First Presbyterian Church
- Grace Presbyterian Church
- Memorial Drive Presbyterian Church
- Servant-Savior Presbyterian Church
- St. Thomas Presbyterian Church

23. Reformed Baptist (1)

 • Grace Family Baptist Church (Spring)

24. Quaker (1)

 • Live Oak Friends Meeting

25. Seventh-Day Adventist (2)

 • Houston International Seventh-Day Adventist Church
 • West Houston Seventh-Day Adventist Church

26. Unitarian (1)

 • Unity of Houston

27. Unity of the Brethren (1)

 • Westheimer Community

28. Vineyard (1)

 • Vineyard Church of Houston

Studying the names of churches is quite interesting. Newer churches tend to go for names beyond the traditional—something innovative and catchy yet conveying a significant message. I admire the creativity expressed in the names!

Among the most trendy I've found is the word *point* or *pointe* compounded with other words, such as BridgePoint, ChangePointe, Clearpoint, Crosspoint (two of these are different denominations), Grace Point, and LifePointe. The use of *bridge* is also popular—the Bridge, BridgePoint, and Faithbridge as examples. The use of the words *faith*, *cross*, and *grace* are abundant, having long been favorites as church names.

The word *fellowship* often replaces the word *church* in a name, but I know of at least a couple of churches that formerly used *fellowship* but have gone back to the word *church*. So many churches are called community churches that some people think it is a denomination. According to my inquiries, that is not the case.

There was a time when every denomination included the denominational name in the official name of their church, such as First Methodist Church. That is no longer true. Often, the name of the denomination is left out, making it challenging to discern these from independent churches.

Some churches, wanting to portray a "nonchurchy" image with more appeal to those with no church background, come up with original titles such as the Ark, the Met, the Bridge, Current, Ecclesia, or Higher Dimension. These have a lot of appeal but can also cause a little confusion—is it a business, a fitness center, a theater, a petting zoo? Well, that's an exaggeration, but the names can be a bit misleading if all a person knows is the name on the sign.

It is common for older churches to be named after a saint, or the name of the neighborhood, their street location, or geographical area. Newer churches with citywide outreach goals shy away from designations that would seem to limit their scope of outreach.

What's in a name? When it is a church name, the name can make a huge difference in how the church is perceived by the general public.

FACTS AND FIGURES

Although I attended 115 worship services as a secret-church-shopper, only 100 churches were selected to obtain the following information.

Mission Statements

Mission statements were observed on exterior signage, posted inside the building, and more often on bulletins and other printed materials. It is possible that other churches did actually have a mission statement but did not display it in a way that could be observed.

- 51 displayed mission statements
- 49 did not display mission statements

Gender of Senior Pastors

- 95 male pastors
- 5 female pastors

Length of Sermons

Someone once said, "There is no such thing as a bad short sermon." After sitting through 115 different types of sermons, I think I agree! Sermons varied greatly in length. I easily timed each sermon with my iPhone stopwatch, from the first word the pastor spoke until the last word.

- 82 minutes (longest sermon)
- 11 minutes (shortest sermon)
- 33 minutes (average length of all)

Invitations/Altar Calls

- 63 offered some kind of invitation to receive salvation
- 37 offered no invitation to receive salvation

Meet and Greet After Church

Some churches invited visitors to a meet-and-greet time with the pastor and/or staff after the service.

- 55 had meet and greet after service
- 45 had no meet and greet after service

Welcoming Visitors and Guests

Most, but not all, churches have a special time during the worship service to welcome visitors. It can be indicated in the bulletin, projected on the screens, announced by the pastor, or all three. The degree of warmth and sincerity expressed at this time is most important. This is that one-chance-to-make-a-good-impression moment.

- 59 extended welcome to visitors during the service
- 41 made no mention of visitors during the service

Being Ignored

It is hard to believe that a person could walk into a church, mill around for thirty minutes, sit in a worship service, hang around another twenty minutes, and not be spoken to at all; I mean, not even a polite hello in passing! I believe it now—it happened to me!

- 47 ignored me completely
- 21 greeted me only at the designated visitor-welcome time
- 37 greeted by more than one person
- 22 did not speak to me unless I spoke first

Oops! Although my preplanned visitor policy was to not speak to anyone until spoken to, sometimes I slipped!

Where First Greeting Occurred

- 11 parking lot
- 42 front door
- 12 lobby
- 2 hall
- 2 classroom
- 17 worship center

Types of Worship Services

I experienced various styles and formats of worship services. Although this is a rather subjective area, I loosely categorized each service in four types.

- 18 formal/liturgical
- 23 traditional
- 33 contemporary
- 26 blended

Multiple Services

Some churches offer multiple services on Sunday mornings. I visited one church that has four morning services: 7:00 a.m., 9:00 a.m., 11:00 a.m., and 1:00 p.m. I attended the 7:00 a.m. service, thinking attendance would be sparse—to my great surprise, it was packed!

- 54 offered multiple Sunday morning services and, in some cases, an identical Saturday evening service
- 46 offered one Sunday morning service

Baptism

Only nine churches baptized on a Sunday when I was present:

- 7 immersed
- 2 sprinkled
- 16 was the most baptized in one service

Welcome Desks

- 56 had some type of welcome desk
- 44 had no welcome desk

Gifts For Visitors

- 34 gave gifts to visitors
- 66 gave no gifts to visitors

In the chapter titled, "Are You Kidding Me?" there is a list of the fifty plus gifts I received.

Visitor Cards

At each church, I made it a *priority* to secure a visitor card, fill it out, and turn it in as instructed.

- 87 visitor cards I turned in
- 13 churches with no visitor card (I requested one at each church.)

Out of the 87 cards I turned in,

- 52 churches contacted me after my visit
- 35 churches never contacted me in any manner

Methods of Contact of the Fifty-Two Churches

- 17 phone calls
- 14 letters
- 20 cards
- 1 personal home visit

Forty churches contacted me more than one time.

Time between My Visit and the Contact

- 2 hours (least amount of time)
- 61 days (longest time)
- 9.4 days (average time between my visit and the contact)

The Lord's Supper

- 32 churches that served communion
- 11 served grape juice
- 9 served wine
- 12 served both to give participants a choice

Church Facilities

In evaluating church facilities, I looked for basic cleanliness and general maintenance. It is not unreasonable to expect every church facility to be clean, orderly, and set up, ready to go on Sunday mornings. On three occasions, I helped church members clean and straighten up a Bible study room, a fellowship area, and a hallway because "there was an event the night before." Not a good thing!

Childcare areas and restrooms should be spotless, ready for the first arrivals on Sunday morning and "spot-checked" throughout the day. Here are my ratings of church facilities:

- 34 are first-class, an A+
- 29 are really nice
- 24 are okay
- 7 really need help
- 6 are poor

3 Ws Grading System for All Churches

Each church was evaluated in three main areas, the 3 Ws—the Word, the Warmth, and the Welcome. Each area has a score range from 1–33. The best grade a church could receive in each W would be 33 points, and the lowest is 0. The points from each W were added together to produce the overall grade, making 99 the highest score possible.

- The Word. Did the sermon magnify Jesus Christ? Was it based on God's Word? And were people given an opportunity to accept Christ as their personal Savior?
- The Warmth. If I were a hurting person in need of help or counseling, did I feel accepted and comfortable enough to ask for help? Did I feel like this was a group of people whom I would like to become close friends with?
- The Welcome. Was I greeted and welcomed in a way that would make me want to come back?

Score of the Churches

- 99 (highest possible score): 10 churches
- 90–98: 35 churches
- 80–89: 10 churches
- 70–79: 4 churches
- 60–69: 5 churches
- 50–59: 7 churches
- 40–49: 7 churches
- 30–39: 6 churches
- 20–29: 6 churches

- 10–19: 3 churches
- Below 10: 7 churches

There are 100 churches total. The average score is 63.

THE PAPER TOOLS

Without a valid system of recording my church-visit findings, it would not be possible to share accurate information. I realized this was of utmost importance in achieving my goal. I developed several simple forms that enabled me to keep a written record of each visit. I refer to the forms I used in putting this book together as my *paper tools*.

Church Evaluation Form (CEF)

Every Sunday afternoon, while the morning's experience was fresh in my mind, I transferred what I had learned to the for-my-eyes-only church evaluation form (CEF), which includes over 150 grading areas. Although this form would not be shared in its entirety with the pastor, it became the basis for compiling what would be shared. After filling out the CEF, it was placed in a large three-ring binder (I wound up with four of these) along with the bulletin and any other printed info gathered on the visit. This process also served as a great memory jogger to recall details of each visit. I must admit that after visiting 100+ churches, they could easily all run together in my mind. Remarkably, every time I opened a binder and found a church entry, it all came back to me with great clarity.

Here is a sample of some of the informational areas included on the CEF:

- Spiritual evaluation—the 3 Ws
- Church contact info
- Pastor's sermon info and grade
- Date and time of visit
- Denomination and mission statement
- Size of church, ethnic makeup, style of service, etc.

- Type of music and instrumentation
- Mode of baptism, Lord's Supper, offerings, invitations
- Method of recognizing visitors, visitors desk, registration forms
- Method of church-visitor follow-up
- Quality and warmth of greeting
- Quality of church facilities

What-in-Heaven Summary Sheet

This form is a summary of the information recorded on the church evaluation form (CEF). Whereas the CEF is only for my benefit, the what-in-heaven summary sheet has an entirely different purpose. This is the form prepared for each pastor as a report of what I experienced while visiting his/her church. After completing all my church visits, a what-in-heaven summary sheet was mailed to all one hundred pastors on the same day, along with a personal letter.

Once again, it is most important to keep in mind that my main goal is to provide firsthand information for the church to advance the kingdom of God. I repeat that here to make it clear that I have no other agenda. I fervently prayed that each pastor would take my comments in the manner that I offered them. Not every what-in-heaven summary sheet contained a glowing report. My intention was not to criticize but to bring out what could be improved in order to advance the kingdom of God.

Pastor Letter

I put a lot of thought and prayer into the wording of the letter to the pastor that accompanied the what-in-heaven summary sheet. I consulted a number of pastor friends who helped me tweak it a bit to come across as supportive, kind, and loving. The last thing I wanted to do was offend the recipient! Knowing how busy pastors are, I also wanted it to be brief and to the point. I did everything I could think of to ensure that this communication would not just be tossed in the trash.

Putting myself in the shoes of the pastor receiving my letter and report, I knew I would probably think, *Who is this guy?* or *I wonder if I met him when he visited?* That's why I had a small photo of myself on the stationery printed for this use.

An equal amount of thought went into the envelope printed especially for this project. I know from experience how much mail can come across a pastor's desk. Hoping to catch the attention and pique the interest of the receiver, the following words were printed on the diagonal just above and slightly left of the address area:

> I visited your church…
> here's what I found out.

At the bottom of the envelope are these words: "What in HEAVEN Is Going On at Church?" Wanting to emphasize a personal touch, I hand addressed each envelope—the form inside was also filled in by hand in the same blue ink.

Feedback Form

The day finally arrived when I mailed out one hundred packets containing the pastor letter and what-in-heaven summary form to churches I had visited. Although I felt the info given on the form was pretty straightforward and self-explanatory, I wanted to make myself available to anyone who might wish to talk. Therefore, a sentence in the pastor letter reads, "Enclosed is a summary of what I experienced at your church. If you would like to discuss this further, please feel free to contact me at (my phone)."

The feedback form was prepared to record the good, bad, and ugly of feedback phone calls I might receive after the mail out to the one hundred pastors. I welcomed this interaction with my fellow pastors. I had prayed that my evaluations would be well received, but I realized it was possible that some might take offense. Whether the reactions to come would be favorable or hostile, it was my intent to receive all graciously.

I had to wait only a couple of days to have the first hint of what was to come. The letters were mailed on a Monday, and two phone calls were received two days later. I was quite anxious to know how helpful my info proved to be and the plan of action each church might take as a result. I received a total of twenty contacts as follows:

Contact	Contacted by
Phone: 16	Pastor: 14
Cards: 3	Staff member: 5
Letters: 1	Elder: 1

All the written responses received were in essence thank-you notes. As to phone calls, I am pleased to say that most were extremely appreciative and open to my remarks. They were glad to be made aware of deficiencies and expressed their intention to correct weaknesses I had discovered in my visit. Some pastors had presented the summary form for review with their staff at the weekly staff meeting.

The above numbers only reflect the feedback that came in response to the mail out. In reality, that was only a small portion of the total feedback. Whenever I received a visitor-follow-up phone call because I had visited the church, I always revealed to the caller that I had come as a secret church shopper. I let them know about the evaluation summary sheet that would be mailed later and the book that I would be writing about my experience.

Most often, these calls came from the pastor or another staff person—who, in every case, expressed great interest in what I was doing and showered me with questions about my assessment of their church. Many lengthy and fruitful conversations about the work of ministry occurred in this informal manner before the summary sheet was ever sent out. Many invitations were extended to meet with their staff or speak to the entire church body upon completion of the project.

One pastor was particularly impressed with the value of what I was doing. So much so that he offered to provide his church facility at no charge and assist with mail outs to invite pastors and their staffs to a gathering to discuss my findings, look at church trends, and to pray to unite the family of God.

An interesting and unexpected outcome—several pastors, each of different denominations, called to say they had heard about what I was doing from a pastor buddy and asked if I would come and secret-shop their church too! Never anticipated referrals!

Whether a pastor chooses to use the information I sent them or not is out of my hands. Perhaps some wound up in the proverbial file 13. But I believe a pastor could not read the information I sent and be neutral about it. It would surely cause him to think, *We have to do a better job in greeting folks*, or *I need to check on our visitor-follow-up procedures*, or even *I am going to pass this report on to my staff.* I consider this a worthwhile response. Even if it is only a little bit of help, praise God for the little bit!

All in all, it has been exciting and rewarding to visit and worship as a secret church shopper with so many different members of the family of God! I am grateful to have had this opportunity. On every visit, I focused on my main goal: to provide firsthand information for the church to advance the kingdom of God.

I can honestly say without hesitation that my motives have been pure, and I have consistently followed my guidelines throughout the project. As a result, I have truly discovered what in heaven is going on at church, at least among 115 churches in the Greater Houston area.

OTHER THOUGHTS

In the mid-1860s, William Carey, at the young age of twenty-two, felt the Lord calling him to the mission field. He left his home in England; and after an extended, arduous journey by sailing vessels, he finally made it to India, exhausted and ill. He knew one other missionary in the entire country, who met him and took him to his home to recuperate, study the language, and pray. After a time of rest and healing, William began his humble ministry.

After a lengthy separation from his wife and children, William sent for them to join him. They too had a rough journey filled with storms at sea, cold, and sickness, but finally they arrived in India. One of his children became ill on the voyage and eventually died.

Enjoying the blessings of God, the ministry Carey established grew strong and fruitful. Eventually, under God's direction, it became a powerful force spanning over fifty years, the effects of which have trickled down even to this day.

Through the years of faithful service, William Carey kept an accurate record of his ministry and a journal of his life's work. In his twilight years, this dedicated lifelong missionary penned this statement in his diary, "I am not afraid of failure; however, I am afraid of success in things that don't matter."

I am sharing information with pastors and churches in the hope that it really does *matter*—because advancing the kingdom of God really does *matter*!

CONCLUSIONS

The more churches I visited as a secret church shopper, the more I learned, and I was fascinated by it all. More importantly, I experienced the presence of God in a new and fresh way—and I stood amazed!

My prayer is that sharing my experiences will serve to benefit and improve the local church so that the entire body of Christ will be enlarged and strengthened.

In assessing 100+ churches, I have seen strong points and weaknesses. Perhaps this one excels above others in one area, and that one is tops in another area. I've had cause to wonder what it would be like to make a composite of all the best in this and the best in that—all the best points rolled up into one big superchurch. Or better yet, what *if* every church had the following:

- Facilities of Second Baptist, Houston (six campuses)

- Landscaping of Chapelwood UMC
- Choir and orchestra of Tallowood Baptist
- Enthusiasm of the Greater Macedonia Baptist Church
- The well-drilling Living Water ministry of Sugar Creek Baptist Church
- Financial freedom of Sagemont Church (debt-free since 1975)
- Ethnic makeup of St. Cyril's Catholic Church
- Kids' Easter egg hunt of Parkway Fellowship North (twenty-five thousand eggs)
- Great coffee and snacks of Gateway UMC
- Spiritual excitement and expression of the Fellowship of the Nations
- Friendliness of the Bridge
- Historic sanctuary of St. Paul's United Methodist Church
- Personal visitation program of Kingsland Baptist Church
- Lighting system of St. Edith Stein Catholic Church
- Commitment to men's ministry of the PowerHouse Church
- Wednesday evening teaching of West Oaks Fellowship
- Relaxed atmosphere of the All-Around Cowboy Church
- Welcome Center of Christ Evangelical Presbyterian
- Vision and commitment to the future of Neartown Church
- Praise dancers of Congregation Beth Messiah
- Parking team of the ARK
- Evangelistic fire of the Church at Bethel's Family
- Packed services of Wheeler Avenue Baptist
- Visitor's Bibles of FaithBridge
- Lord's Supper service of Parkway Fellowship
- Contemporary service of Woodlands Church
- Media capabilities and equipment of Lakewood
- Pipe organ of First United Methodist Church
- A cappella music of First Colony Church of Christ
- Parking lots of Grace Church, Humble
- Mission statement of Berachah

- Saturday morning men's breakfasts of the Church Without Walls
- Classrooms of First Baptist, Pasadena
- Youth ministry of the Community of Faith (Hockley)
- Spanish-speaking service of Grace Community
- Exciting future of LifePointe Fellowship
- Outside cross of Sagemont Church (170 feet tall)
- Dedication to biblical teaching of Memorial Drive Presbyterian
- Lord of the Streets ministry of Trinity Episcopal
- Praise band of CrossPoint (Bellaire)
- The youth facilities of the Met

Wow! How spectacular is that! But wait—what's it really all about? Every church could be all of the above, but if they did not preach *Jesus Christ*, it would all be in vain and mean nothing!

> For this reason we never become discouraged. Even though our physical being is gradually decaying, yet our spiritual being is renewed day after day. And this small temporary trouble we suffer will bring us a tremendous and eternal glory, much greater than the trouble.
> For we fix our attention, not on things that are seen, but on things that are unseen. What can be seen lasts only for a time, but what cannot be seen lasts forever." (2 Corinthians 4:16–18, GNB)

May our focus ever be on the eternal!

7

What About Mission Statements?

In attending 115 church services as a secret church shopper, I found 51 churches that had a mission statement or some type of catchphrase or byline to briefly describe who they are, or some had both. It is common today for all kinds of organizations, businesses, clubs, and other institutions to have a mission statement—so they must be of some value.

But what about mission statements for churches? What purpose do they serve? Are they needed? Are they helpful? Do they make a difference? After a bit of personal research and asking a lot of church members these questions, I have come up with this definition of a church mission statement:

> A brief description of what a church's primary goals and passions are as they grow and strengthen fellow believers while following the Great Commission and sharing Christ's saving grace and love with a lost world.

Now that you have read that definition, please look away from this paper and recite it by memory (pause—tick, tick, tick—time's up!). Well, how did you do? The above definition is a "busy" thirty-five-word statement that could simply be summarized by these seven words: "It defines the purpose of the church."

What good is a church mission statement if no one in the church knows it? I have found that many pastors really believe that their church mission statement is embedded in the hearts and is constantly on the lips of their church members. My inquiries have indicated that the opposite is true. During my visits, I have asked lots of folks these two questions: "Does your church have a mission statement?" and "What is it?" Here is a sampling of answers I have received:

- "I really don't know."
- "I don't think we have one."
- "Isn't that part of the children's ministry?"
- "I think it is printed in the bulletin."
- "I don't think we use it anymore."
- "My kids know it."
- "We dropped it when we moved into the new building."

To those who answered yes to the first question, I then asked if they could quote it. Only 5 percent could do so, 10 percent knew a few words, 15 percent came sort of close, and the remaining 70 percent responded with that deer-in-headlights stare. If the church mission statement is not in the hearts and on the minds of the church body, what good is it? Here are the must elements of a mission statement:

1. State the purpose of the church
2. Reflect biblical authority and truth
3. Represent the passion of the church and their reason(s) for being a church
4. Be short, simple, and spiritually revealing
5. Be easy to memorize—kids too!
6. Be able to connect with all the church ministries while reflecting the common purpose of the church

For example, here is the church mission statement I am most familiar with: "To be living proof of a loving God to a watching world." In this same church, the men's ministry mission statement is "To win men to Christ." When you combine the two, you have,

"To win men to Christ so they can be living proof of a loving God to a watching world."

Do you see how these two mission statements combine to make a powerful statement and express a common purpose of the church?

Here is a mission statement I found in a church bulletin:

> To proclaim the gospel of JESUS CHRIST through worship, service and evangelical outreach: welcoming all people into GOD's family and, in response to GOD's grace, caring for and equipping them for ministry in today's world.

This is a great statement! More power to them! However, how many people will memorize these thirty-five words? Think back to the beginning of this chapter where I wrote a sample definition of a church mission statement. It also contained thirty-five words. Do you recall how you felt as you read it? Get the point? If you were talking to someone about your church, could you recite your church mission statement? Would they be able to get the message and easily understand it? How do you think they would feel if you quoted the previous mission statement to them?

I served on the staff of a megachurch that definitely needed a new mission statement. The one we used had been around a long time, sounded a little out-of-date, and no one could quote the forty-seven words. It required so much space to print that it was seldom in the bulletin, much less spoken of. I wrote it on the inside cover of my Bible so I would have it just in case.

It had been printed on a 3 × 5 rectangular sheet of foam-core board. The board had been displayed around the church, as well as at camps and retreats, for years. It was riddled with nail holes and gummy from sticky-tape residue on the back, making it pretty unsightly. Whenever we had guests, I would make sure it was out of sight and hoped they would not ask me about it. Of course, I was fine if I had my Bible with me!

Obviously, it was time for our church to create a new mission statement. The entire executive staff got prayed up and went off campus for a mission-statement retreat. We met in a room for over eight hours, praying, writing, discussing, and praying some more—and our Lord guided us in writing a new mission statement.

That was just the beginning. There was a well-orchestrated church-wide campaign to teach everyone the new mission statement. This entire process was a God thing. We wrote it in 2005, and the mission statement is as relevant today as the day our Lord revealed it to us. Eighty to ninety percent of the entire church knows it by heart, including the children. It contains twelve powerful and descriptive words. Our mission is, "To be living proof of a loving God to a watching world."

Many powerful things are said in just a few words, and mission statements can be the same. Think about the three words Nike uses that everyone in the entire world seems to know—Just Do It. How about Winston Churchill's famous twenty-five-second speech he gave to the nation of England as they were facing dire circumstances during World War II: "Never, never, never give up!"

If you think about it for just a minute, you will remember some other words, which are the most powerful, influential, and world-changing statements ever spoken by the most powerful Person who ever existed. Jesus said, "I am the way," "Fear not," "I will come again." Some of His followers spoke powerful words when they said, "He is risen." PTL! A few words can pack a punch and go a long way in communicating what needs to be known—especially in church mission statements.

Here are examples of church mission statements and phrases I found in bulletins, on church marquees, and posted on walls in churches I visited:

- A family of believers committed to making disciples of Christ who glorify God in all of life
- Reaching, teaching, and loving all people with the love of Christ

- Building a compassionate community that draws people from all cultures and generations into an authentic, intimate and supernatural life with Christ
- To lead people to discover, develop and deploy their God-given influence for His purpose and glory
- To love and lead ALL people to life change in Christ
- To glorify God by making disciples, equipping families and serving the world with the gospel of Jesus Christ
- To be a dynamic congregation that declares God's Word to our community and beyond: that draws people to Christ; leads people to develop a godly lifestyle; and seeks to demonstrate God's love through service
- Move toward people—move forward—move outward for God
- To evangelize the unbeliever, and through exegetical and expository teaching of Scripture, to enable the believer to fulfill God's plan, will, and purpose for his life
- To make more and stronger disciples of Jesus Christ who make more and stronger disciples of Jesus Christ
- A kingdom-minded, Christ-centered, multi-generational community of faith
- Encourage every person to meet Christ and take the next step with Christ
- Growing in truth...prayer...worship...purpose...for the future...and developing intimacy and power
- God's multi-ethnic bridge that draws all people to JESUS CHRIST who transforms them from unbelievers to missionaries
- Committed in helping build strong families, healthy relationships and providing you a comfortable environment and transformational teachings where your faith in God can grow
- To embody God's grace as we receive it and give it to those who need it

- Moving from self-reliance to total dependence on Christ as we share His life with others
- To bring souls into Christ's church and to nurture their spiritual growth
- Compelled by the love of Jesus Christ and empowered by the Holy Spirit, we carry the gospel to Houston and to the world

In addition to mission statements, some churches use a brief descriptive phrase, more or less like a byline, usually along with the church name. Here are some examples:

- To know Christ and make Him known
- Guiding people to the next step with God
- Finding life—building the future
- Loving God, proclaiming Christ, living generously
- Where Christ comes first
- A church for your family
- A close family in a big city
- Guiding people to the next step with God
- Connecting with God and you
- Making disciples—transforming the world
- Gather, grow, and go
- Discover, develop, and deploy
- A community that gives
- To know Christ and make Him known
- A church for our community
- Where tradition meets tomorrow
- Making sense out of life
- Experience, grow, give, and belong
- Glory to God!
- An authentic, spirit-filled experience
- We are a way of living
- Faith, focus, and finish
- Let's do life together

- Let's love and care for others as Jesus cares for us
- Sharing Christ's light to a dark world
- God's Word, God's people, God's church
- To know and share Christ
- No perfect people allowed
- Everyone needs a little grace @ Grace Church
- Living His name with passion and purpose
- Living God's Word
- Hearts revived—hearts changed
- Church is fun!
- Transformed by faith—transforming through service
- Growing God's people for ministry
- Not your momma's church!

These are a few samples of powerful and meaningful statements. Can you imagine how strong and influential churches would be if each one lived up to their mission description? Defining their mission purpose in words is a giant step toward living up to their claim!

It is imperative that the church leadership know where they are headed, be focused on what they are doing, and that the congregation is made aware of it so they can follow along. It is important for staff and membership to bond together and be on the same page.

A church will certainly not rise or fall because they do or do not have a mission statement. However, it can be an effective tool to help define purpose and unity in ministry. Give it a try!

8

Are You Still Passing the Offering Plates?

When was the last time you ran down to your local Blockbuster store on the corner and rented a VHS? How many times have you used a pay phone in the last year? If you need to make a phone call to someone not in your Contacts list on your smartphone, do you get out your phone book and look up the number? The last time you prepared a paper for a college course, did you use an IBM Selectric typewriter? Did I hear you say, "What's a typewriter?" How many cassette tapes have you listened to lately? Do you still use a flip phone? How about an iPhone—is it a 4, a 5, or a 6?

The point is, times are changing! They have always been changing, but never in the history of mankind have things changed so rapidly. The catalyst for all this change is technology. I was in a meeting not too long ago where the speaker explained how society can just about complete the adjustment to a major high-tech shift—then *boom*, another advancement comes on the scene. This requires letting go of the last new thing and adjusting to the newest thing. To illustrate this point, he made the tongue-in-cheek statement, "No one under forty writes checks anymore." I was grateful I had left my checkbook in the car!

As a young boy, I was taught that I should always give money to the Lord via His church. It made sense to me then and still does. I was also taught to tithe. That also made sense to me. As a young teenager, working part-time at a Dairy Queen for $.65 an hour, I placed 10 percent of each paycheck in an envelope to drop in the offering plate on Sunday. It is a habit I have carried with me to this day.

Yes, I have heard all the arguments about tithing. I know it is only mentioned in the Old Testament, and no one is commanded to tithe in the New Testament. It's been a lot of years since I worked at Dairy Queen, but throughout the years, I have continued regularly giving a minimum of a tithe to the work of the Lord. It works for me, and I enjoy worshiping our Lord by tithing.

However, younger generations often don't know what the word *tithe* means. More than a few times, I have heard folks make a statement similar to this: "I tithe 3 percent of my income." No, by definition, *tithe* means 10 percent. A person may give 3 percent or 23 percent or 33 percent of their income, but that is not considered a tithe—a tithe refers only to 10 percent.

Personal experience has shown me that people who dispute the concept of tithing by pointing out that it was an Old Testament practice usually give far less than 10 percent. Their objection seems to be an attempt to justify the fact that they give in such a meager way. However, when giving in the New Testament is studied, we find the early Christians giving far more than a mere tithe. In fact, according to Acts 2:44–45 (NASB), they "had all things in common; and they began selling their property and possessions and were sharing them with all, as anyone might have need." And again in Acts 4:32–35 (NASB), we read,

> And the congregation of those who believed were of one heart and soul; and not one of them claimed that anything belonging to him was his own, but all things were common property to them.

Verse 34–35 tell us,

> For there was not a needy person among them, for all who were owners of land or houses would sell them and bring the

proceeds of the sales and lay them at the apostles' feet, and they would be distributed to each as any had need.

Clearly, the New Testament sets a much higher standard than the tithing of the Old Testament!

Although I do not believe Jesus expects all believers to sell everything they have to give to the work of His kingdom, I do believe we are to be willing, generous, and even sacrificial givers. Acknowledging all we have is from the hand of God should change our perspective about giving. Nothing is truly ours—it all belongs to Him, and He has made us stewards, as suggested in Luke 12 and 16. May we be found faithful in our stewardship!

For myself, I consider the tithe of the Old Testament as a guideline. If, under the law, God expected 10 percent from His people and the New Testament indicates a higher standard, why would I think God would be pleased with my giving less than 10 percent? According to my giving mind-set, I would never feel comfortable giving less than 10 percent of my income but instead give above the tithe as He leads me to do.

God does not expect anyone to give what they do not have. Some have prospered financially more than others, so their bottom-line amount could certainly be greater. But a percentage applies to all of us! When we consider how much Jesus gave for us, we should be moved to give back—generously. It becomes a tangible way to express our love, gratitude, and worship of Him.

Church people of my generation know all about this giving stuff, and to us, it is no big deal. But new folks coming into the church don't have a clue. Those with no church background may be unfamiliar with how a church operates and certainly do not speak church language. They have no idea about giving to God. So when they are approached about giving to the church, tithing, or signing a pledge card, they are very hesitant. Since they have not been exposed to biblical teaching on giving, some instruction in scriptural giving is in order.

A new survey indicates Americans spend on average 3 percent beyond their means. Maybe teaching good money management is where we need to begin. Good stewardship includes how we handle *all* of what God has provided for us. Out-of-control spending can certainly be a detriment to giving to the work of the Lord. No wonder so many people think they can't "afford" to give!

The fact that church giving is on the decline across the nation has previously been discussed in the chapter titled, "Let's Visit a Church Together: The Service Continues," under the heading "Offering."

The young generations in our churches today, even those who have been around for a while, are basically not givers—they are not motivated to give the same as their predecessors. Why? Many churches may be reaping the consequences of trying to be "user-friendly" for many years. Pastors have been fearful of scaring folks away by talking about money to the extent that these young church attenders are ignorant about giving in any form. They have heard so little about giving that many of them think Mission Board came from *Star Trek* and Lottie Moon is a dress designer! (In case you don't know, Lottie Moon gave her life as an early missionary to China in the 1800s. An annual missions offering is named for her.)

Another factor we are up against is to counteract the prevailing attitude of distrust among millennials in particular. Their skepticism is fueled by media reports of dishonest and unscrupulous pastors in church financial scandals. TV programs abound, featuring charlatan preachers promising outlandish monetary gain and physical healings in exchange for donations, complete with too-good-to-be-true testimonials of miraculous healings and incredible overnight fortunes.

With this deceptive climate in our culture, it is no wonder some young adults find it difficult to open their wallets to the church. They might give a dollar or two for a mission project to build a shelter for street orphans in South America or help drill a clean water well in a remote village in Africa, but they would prefer to see you buy the board and nail it on the frame of the shelter or purchase the shovel and dig the hole themselves. That way, they know that the money they gave to the church mission project is being used for what they gave it for.

As a pastor, I have heard it said so many times, in one form or another, "All that church talks about is money!" or "The only thing that church wants is my money!"

Some churches have deservedly earned that type of negative reputation. During my church visits, I found numerous differences in how churches do church. However, I found *no* churches that did not mention giving an offering to the church! I think it was the one constant factor!

Here is an example of what I consider the wrong way to approach the subject of giving, which could easily contribute to the negative attitude of many toward money and the church. Offering plates were passed three different times in one service for three separate offerings:

1. A "catch-up" offering for the budget
2. Regular Sunday morning offering
3. An offering to raise funds for scholarships for summer youth camp

It felt very awkward to me to have the pastor introduce each offering and make a passionate plea to the folks there to give. It was disturbing when he referred to us in the congregation as being responsible if "Johnny is not able to go to camp." I cannot see that projecting guilt is an acceptable method to motivate giving.

Church garage sales, coupon-book sales, fish fries, auctions, golf tournaments, barbecues, bake sales, and T-shirt promotions are not bad in themselves, and I am sure the funds they raise are important for certain ministries and projects. However, if a church depends on this type of fund-raising to sustain the church, they have the wrong focus, and their church is in trouble.

One of the churches I visited was a large, very formal orthodox church. As I drove into the campus, I immediately noticed a large billboard erected on the property. It was about the size of the ones we see on freeways and highways. The fresh dirt piled around the four large posts on which it was mounted testified to the fact that it had just been installed. It was professionally well-done and eye-catching with a dominant orange color scheme. I thought, *I bet that sign cost a pretty penny.*

I parked, and as I approached the front door, teenagers in orange T-shirts were handing out orange flyers advertising an annual church-wide event. In the foyer, there were volunteer sign-up tables advertised by orange signs. This was obviously a very big deal for this church. Near the end of the service, a pastor came to the podium to enthusiastically promote the event and said, "We need as many volunteers as possible. This is our church's largest annual fund-raiser." I thought, *Wow—their largest fund-raiser? What if it is rained out?* Better to depend upon God's provision through the gifts of His people than to depend upon various carnivals, festivals, and other special projects as the primary source of funds!

A few years ago, a Christ-centered church was adding a much-needed new building to their existing facilities. When word got out that they were going to build, they were inundated by banks and other lending institutions, wanting to handle the financing for the project. This church has been debt-free for many years, and in no way were they going to borrow money to finance the new building. The pastor, a great friend of mine, enjoyed letting these folks know that God would handle the financing.

It is common to see a sign in front of a building under construction with the name of the lending institution financing the building project. It may read something like this: "This building is being financed by the 1st National Bank of Middleton."

However, while the building mentioned above was being built, the church had a large sign erected in front of the construction site as follows:

Financing for this building is provided by our loving God,
through His people, who want to be living proof of Him,

and desire to tell the world that Jesus saves. Chief Architect is God…to Him be the glory!

The sign stayed in place for all twenty months of the construction process. It was fun to see the various reactions!

Church campaigns to sign a pledge card to support the budget were okay for the gray-hair or no-hair generations, but for today's younger generations—forget that! Times have changed, and perhaps it is time to reassess our methods to generate offerings.

When it comes to church finances, the chief goal of any church or charitable organization is not to make money but to serve a particular ministry or mission. However, to serve either effectively, funding is ultimately necessary. What is God's plan to fund a church anyway? We've looked at what the Bible has to say. I have heard a very wise pastor say on more than one occasion, "God's people, given the right information, will usually do the right thing." This seems quite applicable to this question.

God's people (those who are truly born-again believers), given the right information (biblical truth well explained), will usually do the right thing (will joyfully give of their resources out of a loving and grateful heart toward Jesus). It is very simple. It has to be a simple method, or we couldn't do it. Churches are to put Christ first in everything! When Jesus is the main focus and the church is right with Him, He takes care of the church in every way—including financially! When people love God, they give. It is just natural!

Many churches are set up for online giving and online registration for classes and events. Younger adults, as well as older adults, are accustomed to paying bills online, so church contributions paid online fit right in. But that doesn't solve the problem of reluctance to give by the young among us.

Is there an answer to the question, How do churches inspire younger and older demographics to work together in expanding their reach and funding capacity? Is there a method of giving that is relevant to the digital culture? How does a church create a world where there is a place "at the table" for everyone to participate and give? Some say that if a church is going to survive financially and grow over the next decades, they must position themselves around some form of community-based digital giving that empowers all demographics to participate.

We may be familiar with the concepts of GoFundMe, Kickstarter, Smartgiver, Change.org, and others to raise funds or initiate social change through digital media. Let's pause here and talk about "microgiving"—what is it? Simply stated, it is a whole lot of people giving a small (micro) amount of money on a regular basis. Would you rather have one person give $20,000 to your church or have 20,000 people give one dollar? Obviously, there would be more strength in 20,000 people in a number of different ways.

Microgiving can work in a similar manner as a multilevel marketing plan, except no product is being sold. Instead, an individual pledges to give $1.50 per month to a particular cause. Then they send digital messages to all their contacts describing the ministry they are passionate about and ask their network of contacts to also give $1.50 per month. This second layer of folks are to reach out to their network for $1.50 per month, and so it goes. For such a minimal contribution, most folks are willing to join in out of loyalty to their friend—"if Joe is passionate about this ministry, I want to get on board too." Beginning with a "micro-amount" each month, the numbers can grow exponentially in a relatively short period of time, creating a steady, ongoing revenue stream for the cause.

The 20-80 principle comes into play in church giving. It is well-known in church circles that 20 percent of the people in the church give 80 percent of the money. No matter what kind of research you conduct or how hard you try to disprove or debunk this principle, basically it holds true. For years, many churches have depended on a handful of dedicated church members, some with deep pockets who tithe and give regularly to keep their church budgets in the black. A church will not sustain itself or survive depending on

CEOs. There are wealthy, godly CEOs who give regularly and are a blessing to their church and the family of God. God bless these CEOs! But there is another group of CEOs—the Christmas-and-Easter-only crowd. They are present twice a year and offer little. As I have already mentioned, one pastor told me, "We are about three funerals away from closing our doors."

A while back, I read a book titled *Bowling Alone* by Robert D. Putman (2000). The book lists about thirty-five entities or organizations (YMCA, country clubs, VFW, the church, the Oddfellows, drive-in movies, bowling leagues, Knights of Columbus, unions, political organizations, etc.) that are slowly declining and dying. The book is not written from a Christian perspective (which was a difficult read for me) and goes into great detail about their history, why they were established, their best years, membership, fluctuations in their ranks, and their primary thrusts and purposes. Where are the energetic joiners they had prior to the 1970s? Many of these organizations have been steadily declining since then. Why? Mr. Putman explores the results of an American society that is becoming more alienated and disconnected from families, neighbors, and communities and the effects this has on our society.

The results of Putman's research list the major reasons for the decline of various organizations, and, in some cases, their total collapse. There are some common denominators of failure relative to all organizations. Putman found that they began to fail and decline because of the following:

1. They did not change their purpose in keeping with the times.
2. Through the years, their purpose became irrelevant.
3. They did not bring young members in and train them to lead.
4. Their methods were antiquated and out-of-date.
5. They failed to keep up with technology changes.

There are others, but these five points are an appropriate example to illustrate my points. Organizations committed these obvious mistakes. Their individual histories were full of "did nots," "should haves," and "did not realizes" that eventually led to, and continue leading to, their demise and inevitable collapse. The population of the organization began to age and eventually pass on, and there were no systems in place to replace their members. And there were no adequate up-to-date funding strategies incorporated during their changing times.

This same scenario can be applied to churches today. One of the greatest challenges for churches is to get new folks in the church and then teach them to love Jesus, and they will become givers for the right reasons. The proper term in the secular world is *donor acquisition*. That is a huge challenge for all churches and nonprofit organizations in the country today. Let's look at the facts:

- There are over 1.5 million nonprofit organizations in the United States.
- About $410 billion dollars are contributed annually to non-profits.
- Three demographics of people make up the $410 billion: millennials, baby boomers, and builders.
- 80 percent of those donations come from individuals over the age of 49.
- 10,000 of the individuals ages 49 and above are retiring each day.
- 1000 of the individuals ages 49 and above are dying each day.

I recently read a 334-page Bantam book titled *Sam Walton, Made in America: My Story*. This is the autobiography of Sam Walton, who parlayed a single dime store in a hardscrabble cotton town into Wal-Mart, the largest retailer in the world. In this quite fascinating read, Mr. Walton shares his secrets of success. Godly principles such as honesty, hard work, and fair play were evident. Putting the customer first, making his employees a part of the company, and an immeasurable vision, coupled with high energy, were all ingredients of his success.

However, one habit he constantly practiced was to learn what was happening with his competition and what the new trends in the retail-discount business were. He made herculean efforts to find out what new and innovative products were being developed and what new business practices were on the horizon. Then he always put Wal-Mart in a position to adopt and capitalize on them. Using this method, by the time his competitors found out what Sam Walton was doing, they were already far behind. Much of Wal-Mart's success can be credited to this business strategy and ploy.

Obviously, a man with his credentials and superior business skills knew the downfalls that businesses could face. In the last chapter of his book, "Wanting to Leave a Legacy," on page 324, Mr. Walton refers to one of the most difficult challenges Wal-Mart continually faced: "But all this [referring to Wal-Mart's success] requires overcoming one of the most powerful forces in human nature: the resistance to change. To succeed in the world, you have to change all the time."

In the world of business, if a company doesn't change, they will eventually be attending their own funeral. The same could be true with our churches. We must stay on top of things on all levels of the culture around us to be effective, efficient, and attractive to our "customers" and thereby advance the kingdom of God.

Do we encounter in our churches the resistance to change Sam Walton spoke of? A resounding "you bet" is the certain answer! Resistance most often comes from the membership but can also be prevalent among leadership too. Many pastors and elders are reluctant to depart from "the way we've always done it."

Perhaps a clarification to the realm of change may be in order here. The truth of scripture never changes—the message of the gospel must always remain the same. But the manner in which the whole unchanging counsel of God is presented must be open to continual evaluation and modification. And all things must be directed by the head of the church, Jesus Himself.

A recent article in Forbes Magazine states, "The most successful nonprofits are betting that digital giving is the way of the future and that millennials will lead the way." Read this statement again and substitute the word *church* for *nonprofits*. Could this be the wave of the future?

Many of the tech-savvy among us feel it is past time that churches consider raising funds through a community-based software platform. How can a church leverage their existing database and train people to organize a group of "loyal followers" who share their overall godly vision with others? They say that when you combine a person who is passionate about the cause of Christ and their church's outreach, with the resources to share that passion with others, what transpires is a cooperative compounding effect that spreads organically.

I recently attended a gathering of church and nonprofit leaders for the launch of a Christian microgiving company called GoLoyal, the world's first such entity exclusively catering to charitable organizations and churches, helping them build real-time communities that empower their loyal followers to embrace a role in leadership. Their software allows each member to see their ripple effect from their word-of-mouth and social-media-driven efforts as they share their vision with others.

They are a multichannel answer to fund-raising. They use an innovative, "evolved-giving" system that engages a church's loyal followers to generate a revenue stream through word-of-mouth/peer-to-peer interactions while harnessing web-based technology and social networking to create community and capture donations. This simple, easy-to-use platform allows each member to track the individual and overall impact their efforts are making via a periodic report summarizing downline giving.

Unlike online funding systems that focus on reaching specific project goals, this platform is uniquely aimed at cultivating a steady-growing monthly residual income for churches and other nonprofits.

Please hear what I am saying. In no way am I suggesting that microgiving should replace the biblically based plan of giving to support the church budget. Church funding should be from an outflow of love for Christ. I am just sharing another way to give that is easy for people to understand and relates to a younger high-tech-driven generation. It has been suggested that a program of microgiving could fund specific projects within the church; for example, a mission trip, pastor-retirement fund, or outreach to the homeless.

It is too early to know what effects microgiving might have in the overall realm of church finances. Time will tell, and perhaps the Christian nonprofit world stands to benefit more than the church. Other efforts to educate and motivate believers to give must continue. I am not ready to endorse or renounce the microgiving concept for any kind of church funding. Microgiving may or may not play a significant role in church giving, but we would all do well to be aware of what it has to offer in the way of potential. It is something to think about and prayerfully consider.

The bottom line of giving as far as I am concerned is—no matter how you cut it or explain it or deal with it, giving is still all about loving God!

9

Denominations—Is There a Common Denominator?

THE STORY OF NANCY C.

In my first semester as a high school sophomore, I met a girl in history class named Nancy C. Everyone called her that, even the teachers, because her last name had about eighteen letters in it. No one could even pronounce it, much less spell it. To say that she rang my bell would be an overwhelming understatement! She was a lovely Italian girl whose beautiful long black hair, olive skin, and sparkling eyes literally captured me.

Over a period of weeks, I made an effort to get to know her, and finally my efforts paid off to the point that I asked her if I could take her to an upcoming football game. I knew she had to attend the game because she was a member of the school all-girl drill team, and they were required to be at every home game. She told me she had to ask "Mama and Papa" and would let me know what they said.

A few days later, she told me Mama had said yes. Wow! However, Mama stipulated that she wanted to talk to me face-to-face. Nancy C. then informed me that the drill team had to be at the game two hours early to rehearse their halftime dance routine. I would have to pick her up at 4:30 p.m. to get to the football stadium at 5:00 p.m. because the game started at 7:00 p.m. I thought that was cool because our time together would be that much longer. I suggested that after the game we could go to Prince's Drive-In for a bite to eat. She was agreeable to that but let me know she would have to go back home after the game to change clothes. Drill team members were not allowed to go anywhere in their uniforms except to the game and back. That's okay. I'm cool with it—anything to be with Nancy C.!

The day before my big date, I washed the family car, making sure it was extra clean for Nancy C. As a final touch to impress the girl of my dreams, I sprinkled aftershave lotion all around inside!

On Friday afternoon, I arrived at Nancy C.'s house right on time. I knocked on the front door, and Nancy C. appeared. There she was in all her splendor, outfitted in her drill team uniform. Her first words were, "Mama wants to talk to you." I entered the rather dark living room, where the smell of burning candles was heavy. I quickly noticed that the only light in the living room was produced by candles.

As my eyes adjusted to the semidarkness, I peered into a space filled with items and images that were not the common decor of homes I had visited before. I got an eerie feeling as I tried to take it all in. On the walls and arranged on tables were pictures of Jesus, statues of saints (I guess that's who they were), rosary beads, a statue of a lady whom I assumed represented the Virgin Mary, and a photo of a pope. On one wall hung an oversized picture of Jesus with a gold halo around His head, wearing a white robe and a large red heart on his chest. I felt like He was staring right at me!

Nancy C. told me to wait here, and she would get Mama and Papa. She emerged with her parents in just a few moments. I smiled, introduced myself, and extended my right hand, just like I had practiced. Neither Mama nor Papa shook my hand. Instead, Mama looked me straight in the eye and said in a heavy Italian accent, "Nancy says you are a nice boy...but not a Catholic...we have never let her go out with a boy that was not a Catholic. You can go, but be back before eleven, okay?" The only thing I knew to say was, "Okay." Nancy C. whispered to me, "Papa doesn't speak English." Mama and Papa exited the candlelit room. Feeling a great deal of relief, I headed for the door along with Nancy C.

We made it to the stadium on time, and I discovered pretty quickly the shine of this evening was dimming a bit as I sat in the bleachers for ninety minutes, watching the drill teams of both schools practice and practice and practice. Although I wanted to keep my eyes on Nancy C. the whole time, I had difficulty because all the drill team girls looked alike in their green, gold, and white uniforms.

Finally the drill squads exited, and the football teams that had been warming up on the sidelines took the field and began their pregame warm-up. I headed over to where the drill team was seated to be with Nancy C., only to receive another disappointment. The drill squad had to sit together through the entire game, but we would be able to talk at halftime. As it turned out, that conversation didn't happen either. It seemed that it was Nancy C.'s night to serve on the "props team"; meaning, she was one of a group responsible for getting all the halftime props together after the halftime show. And wouldn't you know—after the game, the props team had to load the props on a bus, take them back to the school, and put them away in the band room. What? Why didn't I know all this before?

After the fourth quarter ended, I watched as the girls took forever loading the props on the bus. Then Nancy C. rode the bus back to the school while I followed behind in my vehicle, thinking the aftershave sprinkled in the car was a waste! My patience was admittedly wearing a little thin as I endured another lengthy wait for the girls to unload the props.

Finally Nancy C. finished her responsibility and met me at my car. I noted the time as 9:45 p.m. as I vividly recalled Mama's words—"before eleven." Next item on the agenda: take Nancy C. home to change out of her uniform. I walked her to the door but opted to wait outside the house. I just couldn't face all those statues looking at me (especially Jesus in the white robe) and smelling that candle smoke again!

A long time ago, I quit trying to figure out why it takes a woman so long to get dressed. The occasion with Nancy C. was one of my early experiences in observing this female phenomenon—Nancy C. definitely fit the mold. At last she walked out the door, giving me another wow moment as I admitted to myself that it was worth the wait!

We headed for Prince's Drive-In. In those days, it was where all the cool people hung out. They offered curb service and had great food, but the best part was "being seen," and I was eager to "be seen" with Nancy C. I parked under the canopy. The carhop arrived, and we ordered fries and two chocolate malts. I felt like Cinderella was sitting in the front seat with me—it was 10:25 p.m., and time was running out.

Engaging in small talk laced with a lot of laughs, I was having a great time, and it seemed like she was too. From my vantage point seated in the driver's seat and Nancy C. in the passenger's seat, I noticed that her left hand was resting on the seat between us. How handy was that! I really wanted to hold her hand, so I took a deep breath and made my move—it was the first "move" I had ever made. With my right hand, I reached over and gently took her hand in mine. She jerked her hand away from me, slapped my hand, and shouted, "Don't touch me, I'm Catholic!"

I was in shock! At a loss as to what I should do next, I flashed my headlights to signal the carhop, paid the bill, and drove straight to her house. Not a word was spoken nor a glance exchanged all the way back. I parked in front of her house, opened the car door for her to get out, and escorted her to the front door. I looked at my Timex wristwatch and found it was 10:55 p.m. As we reached the entrance, Nancy C. said, "I don't think you should come in." I nodded in complete agreement, said good-bye, and returned to my car—the one with the lingering aftershave aroma. It was a night I will never forget! By the way, we lost the game 64-0!

That was my introduction to the Catholic Church. My Nancy C. experience had a negative influence on me for a long time with regard to Catholics. I could not forget the spooky atmosphere of that house. Thinking they were a little weird, I was afraid to even talk to someone who was Catholic—and for sure, I would never try to hold a Catholic's hand!

Over a period of years, whether in casual conversations or in deep counseling sessions, I have heard many people express negative attitudes toward a particular denomination based on a bad experience from their past. Some had been deeply hurt because of a disagreeable situation in a church where they were a member. As a result, they left and vowed never to be a part of that brand of church again. Others have been turned off to a certain denomination due to a scandalous, highly publicized incident of immorality by a pastor. Or it might be that overbearing, self-righteous, Christian-in-name-only neighbor who sours a nonchurch person against a particular denomination.

Far too many people have had a Nancy C. experience in their lives, creating ill feelings, suspicions, and misconceptions that can affect them in a negative way for years. It is not uncommon to find within any congregation a few mauled Methodists, beat-up Baptists, confused Catholics, pounded Presbyterians, lonely Lutherans, crushed charismatics, angry Anglicans, or—well, you get the picture! As a pastor, I cannot count the number of times I have heard somebody say, "I'll never set foot in a _____ (denomination) church again!" We've got a bunch of wounded folks out there!

Have you ever thought about why many churches today do not place the name of their denominational affiliation on their signage or printed materials? It is primarily to eliminate the "turnoff" a potential church member might have to that denomination. Isn't this a bit dishonest? Are we misleading the public about who we are? Or are we just removing a barrier that might hinder a spiritually needy person from a right relationship with God?

From my recollection, it was Rick Warren, pastor of Saddleback Church in California, who pioneered this approach. In canvasing the neighborhood where Rick intended to plant the new church, he asked questions like, "What is it that keeps you from attending church?" or "What are things about church that you do not like?" Among many other insights gained, Rick Warren discovered that lots of stay-home-on-Sunday-morning people had a Nancy C. story in their background. The solution? Don't broadcast your denomination. Pave the way for seekers to leave behind their bad experiences and check out for themselves what the church is really like. After they feel comfortable with the people and the ministry, they are likely to remain open to it even after they learn the denomination. When the denominational name was removed, the hindrance was removed.

WHICH CHURCH IS WHAT DENOMINATION?

I have designed this little match game. Simply match the church name on the left with the denomination name listed on the right by placing the letter of the correct answer in the blank.

Church Name	Denomination
_____ Grace Pointe	A. United Methodist
_____ FaithBridge	B. Lutheran
_____ Freedom Fellowship	C. Bible Church
_____ Cross Point	D. Assembly of God
_____ Bridge Point	E. Presbyterian
_____ Parkway Fellowship	F. Independent
_____ Life-Point	G. Baptist
_____ Bethel	H. Pentecostal

Except for a lucky guess, you could not really know the correct answers! However, the truth about which is which can only be discovered if you visit them yourself. Even then, you would probably have to ask to find out, like I did on my visits. This is just a little activity to illustrate how easy it is to conceal the denomination of the church when it is not a part of the church name and, in doing so, remove the barrier that may be keeping some people away.

My home church is one of those that stopped including the denominational name in the church name. We have heard many stories of people, now faithful members, who would not have made that first visit otherwise. I've had the personal joy to hear some say, "I swore I'd never set foot in a _____ (denomination) church, but here I am, and I love it!"

For an already-established denominational church to change their church name can be a little tricky. There will likely be longtime church members who will initially oppose such a change. Great care must be taken by the leadership over a long period of time to prayerfully and carefully educate the flock as to the purpose. Much better to lovingly bring the congregation into agreement than to arbitrarily make the decision and announce, "Here's what we're going to do." We want to attract the unchurched world to a healthy, harmonious church, not one that is divided and angry!

I know of only a few established churches that have made a name change to exclude the name of the denomination. In most cases, it occurs with a new church start—in fact, it seems to be a trend to do so. In a conversation about this with the head of a large denominational association, he told me, "I can't think of any of the new churches we have started in the last ten years that used our denominational name on their signage." Just based on my church visits, this trend holds true for a few denominations but not across-the-board for all. A glance at the denominational list of churches I visited in the chapter titled "Lists, Facts, Figures, and Paper Tools" will confirm this.

In a casual conversation with a staff person of a very large church, he shared with me their experience with the church name. The church was originally established and had long been known as _____ _____ (denomination) Church. In more recent years, they sometimes referred to the church as the Church at _____, leaving out the denomination. Thinking the latter name had a broader appeal and a more current sound to it, they began using it verbally and on many printed pieces and promotional materials. They continued to use both names interchangeably, even a dual listing in the phone book, though their major signage retained the original name.

Eventually, this became not only confusing but began to create problems. The leadership decided they needed to make a decision as to which name to use—two different names was not a good thing. Interestingly, they opted to hire an outside company to take a survey within the community (not within the church membership) for their input or preference. Wanna guess which way the unchurched community voted?

When I heard the answer, I was not at all surprised—in fact, I had difficulty holding my tongue. My first thought was, *I could have saved you the money it took to hire the polling group!* Thankfully, I was able to keep my thought to myself. Of course, the outside community favored the denominational name included in the church name, _____ _____ (denomination) Church! Why? They want to know the brand up front so they can avoid ever going there if that denomination was the source of their Nancy C. experience. To me, the outcome of the survey only confirms what has previously been discussed.

I have observed another trend that could be, at least in part, a result of the Nancy C. mind-set. A number of new church plants are started as independent churches—they have no denominational affiliation at all. Being a one-of-a-kind independent means no bad history to live down in the minds of potential members.

On the other hand, the trend could be due to the Nancy C. experience of the pastor himself. I know for a fact there are some pastors who have left their own denomination due to conflict and have gone on to start an independent church. "Wounded pastors" is a category that could be added to the list of denominational casualties.

I know of a church that describes itself on their website as an independent church with three "voluntary affiliations with other similar-minded churches." They list an affiliation of structure, an affiliation of values, and an affiliation of mission, the first two being parachurch groups and the third being a mainstream denomination.

Some of the greatest surprises of my church-visiting project have come from visits where I've encountered practices generally not perceived to be the norm for that denomination.

I have attended churches of all sizes with no denomination on the sign that presented great Bible preaching to diverse congregations where people were baptized, the Lord's Supper was observed, there was a wonderful prayer time, people heard a clear salvation message, the music was God-honoring—making it just a great all-around service. Upon exiting, I would stop by the welcome desk, and in the course of our conversation, I would ask *the* question, "Is your church a denominational church or an independent church?" I was often startled by the answer because what I had just experienced in their worship service was not what I thought was characteristic of their denomination.

For example, I visited a United Methodist Church (I had to ask to find out because the church name did not indicate denomination) that baptized by immersion. How can this be? Methodists are known for sprinkling! When the pastor called me to follow up my visit, I questioned him about it. He replied, "We try to follow the Bible rather than our denomination." Amen to that!

I had a rather embarrassing situation occur (although it ended well) when I visited a Church of Christ. As I was driving home, I noticed I had accidentally walked out with one of their hymnals in my hand. These are the people who are known for not using any musical instruments in their services. I suspect they use hymnals to have the advantage of the musical notes to follow for singing in four-part harmony. I can vouch that their a cappella sound is amazing!

The next day, I called the pastor to confess my error and asked if I could just drop it by at a later time. When I returned the songbook, I had an opportunity to visit with the pastor. I explained to him about my secret-church-shopper visits and my book that was in process. Beyond that discussion, I engaged him in conversation about the absence of musical instruments in the Church of Christ. He was very kind and explained their church stance regarding musical instruments.

As we were saying our good-byes, he mentioned there was a Church of Christ in the city that offered both kinds of services. Their early service was a cappella, and the later one featured a praise band. A few Sundays later, I visited the church he referred to and was able to see and hear their music for myself. It is a very large church, and they presented two wonderful services. The early service included the traditional Church of Christ a cappella singing (absolutely beautiful!), and an equally effective praise band was featured at the second service.

I find it interesting that on the bulletin of this same Church of Christ it states, "An independent, nondenominational church." However, printed on the top portion of all their literature is "Church of Christ."

I was greatly encouraged by some comments of a young pastor of a large and dynamic church with no denominational name attached. It was during the phone call he made to me after I visited his church. Upon learning of my mission, we had quite a lively and lengthy conversation. I asked *the* question and learned that they were a United Methodist Church. He told me, "I go to all my denominational meetings and listen to what they have to say. I visit with other pastors and listen to what they have to say. I don't say much. Then I go back to my church and listen to what the Bible has to say. That's what I really go by." Praise God for that! By the way, his sermon and everything about his church worship service were outstanding!

A pastor who will stand with the Word of God and not bend to church traditions or denominational pressure is a breath of fresh air in a polluted world! I have rejoiced to find more than I would have expected of young, as well as seasoned, pastors with a determination to preach the undiluted pure milk of the Word—and they are found in many different denominations as well as independent churches!

Lest it sound like I'm talking against denominationalism or advocating bucking the denominational establishment, let me make it clear that I am a *denomination guy* all the way. There is great strength in joining together with other like-minded individuals to perform the work of ministry. Churches voluntarily aligned with other churches present a united front against the enemy of our souls! Mission endeavors flourish when there is the solidarity of joint outreaches to win the world. Financial resources stretch further when combined with other churches in a cooperative effort to support multiple ministries. There are huge advantages to not going it alone! I would advocate severing denominational ties only in extreme circumstances!

Through fifty years of ministry, I have witnessed wonderful, healthy ministries functioning effectively with denominational leadership—that is most encouraging! Denominational agencies and organizations have trained workers, assisted in church plants, provided resources to sustain vital projects, and done other outstanding work to advance God's kingdom. These are good things!

The word of caution is this: follow the Bible! God's Word is our sole authority. If denominational traditions, practices, or mandates contradict the clear teachings of the Bible, choose the Bible way every time. Jesus established His church—He calls the shots!

A couple of terms usually turn up in news coverage of a political nature, whether it is TV, radio, or newspaper news reports. The terms are conservative and liberal, also known as right wing and left wing respectively. There are certain denominations that are known as being conservative in their theology. Then there are other denominations that are often referred to as being liberal in their theology.

In addition, there is frequently a conservative element as well as a liberal element within the same denomination. I have noticed that, across denominational lines, there may be more doctrinal agreement among the conservatives of a number of different denominations than there is between the conservatives and liberals of the same denomination. In other words, I might identify more closely with conservatives of another denomination than with liberals of my own denomination.

My church visits took me to multiple churches of the same denomination. For example, I visited thirty Baptist churches, ten Methodist, eight Presbyterian, and four Episcopal churches, to name a few (for a complete list, see the chapter titled "Lists, Facts, Figures, and Paper Tools"). Although the average visitor may not be able to easily detect the difference, especially in one visit, I could readily sense the doctrinal leanings from one denomination to the next and from church to church of the same denomination. This is just another way churches may be divided into categories.

One of my church visits was to a denominational church with a reputation of being pretty liberal. I had been acquainted with a wonderful man who was a longtime member of this church until his death a few years back. I could clearly remember this gentleman telling me years ago, "I used to be a Baptist, but they're too strict. So I joined this church, and it fits me."

I was interested to see for myself what it was really like in this "not-so-strict" church that was dubbed as liberal. Their Sunday morning schedule consisted of two worship services with Bible study classes in between. I arrived just as the early service was letting out. The greeter who met me at the door explained the schedule. I expressed my desire to attend a Bible study class and learned from the greeter that there were two adult classes to choose from. The greeter said, "One class is about current events, and the other studies the Bible." I chose the "studies the Bible" class.

Upon reaching the classroom, filling out a visitor card, and getting my coffee, the teacher of the class asked me, "Have you ever been to our church before?" After I answered, he said, "We are a very liberal church, but in this class, I teach right from the Bible." The question came to my mind—since he was obviously a student of the Bible (his teaching revealed this to be true) and had great reverence for the scriptures—why would he want to be a part of this liberal church?

I attended the late worship service after Bible study and found that the church indeed lived up to their liberal reputation. The sermon was definitely not a Bible-based message, and I could not tell you the main point the pastor was trying to make. Frankly, I was bored out of my head, along with the other forty or so people present. Judging by the rather large auditorium and campus size, I would say this congregation has dwindled greatly in numbers.

After enduring the service, I thought back to my question about the Bible study teacher. Instead of wondering why he stayed on at this admittedly liberal church, I thanked God that he chose to remain. He is desperately needed! I pray that God will use this teacher to bring Life to a lifeless church!

I have occasionally wondered why conservatives are referred to as the right and liberals as the left. Then I came across this verse from Ecclesiastes that may shed some light on the origin of the terms.

> The heart of the wise inclines to the right, but the heart of the fool to the left. (Ecclesiastes 10:2, NIV)

I don't really know if that verse is the answer, but it makes all kinds of sense to me! Just sayin' (think smiley face here!).

I did a bit of research to determine the number of different denominations that exist, knowing that this would be a difficult figure to pin down. After contacting several city offices and consulting with a few denominational agencies, the best I could come up with for the Greater Houston area currently is about thirty-six registered denominations. The Pew Forum on Religion & Public Life reports that, as of 2011, there were approximately forty-one thousand Christian denominations worldwide. That is a staggering figure!

I have long believed that denominations can be a huge dividing force among the family of God and therefore a hindrance to the work to which Christ has commissioned us. Having been reinforced by 115 church visits, today I believe this to be true more than ever.

Most of us would probably agree that denominations are man-made. When we get to heaven, we will not be asked about our church brand. Denominational labels will have melted away—only our affiliation with Jesus Christ will matter! We will all be known simply as the family of God.

So why did man come up with this denomination thing anyway? Even during Jesus's stay on earth, we see various factions within Judaism—Sadducees and Pharisees being the most prominent. Paul exhorted the Corinthians, "That you all agree and that there be no divisions among you." They were quarreling, some saying they were of Paul or of Apollos or of Cephas or of Christ. Paul admonished them with the words, "Has Christ been divided?"

Without the intervention of Paul, would the Corinthian church have separated from one another into various factions? There were other disputes and disagreements within the early church. Some of the issues had to do with which days are appropriate for worship, keeping the Sabbath, eating meat sacrificed to idols, and which widows to take care of using church finances. Perhaps we can chalk it all up to our fallen human nature!

DENOMINATIONS—IS THERE A COMMON DENOMINATOR?

We are all familiar with the prayer Jesus prayed the night before He died on the cross. Recorded in John 17, it is a well-loved passage of scripture, made more precious by the fact that Jesus actually included us in His prayer, along with His disciples: "I do not ask on behalf of these alone, but for those also who believe in Me through their word" (John 17:20).

And what was it that the Savior prayed for us in His longest recorded prayer? "That they may all be one…that they may be one…that they may be perfected in unity" (vv. 20–21, 23). Why did Jesus so desperately desire this oneness among His followers? "So that the world may believe that You sent Me...so that the world may know that You sent Me, and loved them, even as You have loved Me" (vv. 21, 23). Would you agree that we have seriously strayed from the unity for which Jesus so earnestly prayed that night long ago?

Anything that divides the family of God is bad! Denominations can do this! Denominations have divided us! Denominations weaken our impact in a world that is rapidly spiraling downward! I personally believe it *doesn't* have to be that way! After all, Jesus prayed that we "may be perfected in unity." It can be done!

The important thing is that we agree on essential matters. That would include things like the nature of God, the deity of Jesus Christ, His sacrificial death on the cross to atone for our sin, His bodily resurrection—His salvation freely offered by His grace and received through our faith. This is how we are born again into God's family. Once we're part of the family, there may be differences over nonessential matters, but those can be set aside in the interest of oneness. Would we be willing to overlook trivial differences to unite with believers with whom we are in agreement on major theology? Could we reach out to other denominational friends to achieve the oneness that Jesus longingly prayed for?

I strongly believe denominations should be more open to one another—love, kindness, and acceptance are desirable qualities in this context. In the minds of the unsaved in our world, we as the church are all lumped together. When outsiders see divisiveness within our ranks, we have lost our influence—all of us! What did Jesus say would be the identifying factor by which the world would recognize His followers? "By this all men will know that you are My disciples, if you have love for one another" (John 13:35). Are we showcasing a "love for one another" that will draw the lost to Him?

As I visited churches of various denominations, I found a number of them outside my own denominational preference where I felt a true kinship! It was one of the greatest joys of my entire project! If I had not seen a sign or been told the denominational connection, I would never have known. We were on the same page in the areas that really matter. Without hesitation, I could easily join forces with these brothers and sisters in Christ to present a united front in winning the world for Christ! Just think how much more effective we could be if we truly stood together! We would do well to proactively work toward that goal!

With some denominations I know, there may be some diversity of thought about secondary issues, but I'd rather not get bogged down in nonessentials. That's where the barriers get in the way and become a detriment to our mission. I could easily lock arms with these denominations to carry out joint ministry projects. What a huge witness to the world this could be! There are few, if any, denominational distinctions on the foreign mission field. It is common for missionaries to work side by side, supportive of the Christian ministries of others. We would do well to follow their lead wherever we minister. Considering how few of us there are, we need to stick together to make an impact for the kingdom!

Denominations were certainly not an issue when hurricanes Katrina and Ike pummeled the Texas Gulf Coast, leaving thousands of people with immediate physical needs. In an emergency situation like this, everyone was needed to assist. Whether helping with food distribution, locating temporary housing, or sorting donated clothing in the name of Jesus, lots of people were needed. I really didn't care about the denominational affiliation of the volunteers. There was a desperate need, and we worked together to meet it.

However, we must be aware that there are some denominations/religious groups whose theology is in direct opposition to the Word of God. To participate along with them would mean, by implication, that we endorse their beliefs. Some of these organizations have names that include the word church, but measured by New Testament teachings, they fall short. If we do not share the same basic tenets of the faith, recognizing Jesus as Lord and realizing His amazing salvation by grace, how could we join together for the purpose of ministry? Sadly, according to their theology, these folks are not even in the family of God!

Does this mean I do not love and care for them? Absolutely not! My calling is to love them and pray for them—pray for their salvation first and foremost. Treat them with respect and grace. The separation we observe is only for the work of ministry. Whereas a friendly relationship on a personal level is certainly acceptable and even commendable, aligning myself with their so-called church for any endeavor is not.

Everything I speak, everything I do, every place I go—all shout in a loud voice what I am all about, and I am all about *Jesus*! By His grace, may it ever be evident to all!

The main focus of the church must be Jesus! His supremacy must be evident in the lives of the church collectively and its members individually. We must be more concerned with the position of Christ in our churches and personal lives than our denomination. Jesus must be lifted up in everything! Jesus is our Common Denominator!

If I could just bust out in song right now, it would be this Bill and Gloria Gaither favorite—"The Family of God"!

Chorus
I'm so glad I'm a part of the family of God
I've been washed in the fountain, cleansed by His blood!
Joint heirs with Jesus as we travel this sod,
For I'm part of the family, the family of God.
Verse 1
You will notice we say "brother and sister" 'round here,
It's because we're a family and these are so near.
When one has a heartache, we all share the tears,
And rejoice in each victory in the family so dear.
Verse 2
From the door of an orphanage to the house of the King,
No longer an outcast, a new song I sing.
From rags unto riches, from the weak to the strong,
I'm not worthy to be here, but praise God I belong!

When we enter the gates of heaven, it will not matter what church we belonged to on earth. All that will matter is that we have accepted Christ as our personal Lord and Savior to become part of the family of God!

10

Where Is Prayer in Our Churches?

The topic of prayer is a subject very close to my heart. The purpose of this chapter is to share insights about how prayer is being utilized in churches today. But more than that, I want to motivate all of us within the body of Christ to grasp the importance of prayer and really pray—not just talk about prayer or become more knowledgeable about prayer but to actually become a people of prayer! It would transform our churches! Godly leaders lead on their knees, and so do effective churches!

When I visited the first church as I began my project, I had all kinds of hopes and expectations of churches in the area of prayer. Since prayer is so vitally important, shouldn't it be obvious? Prayer is the most powerful ministry in the church; it is the connection between us and the Source of all power. Churches that are devoted to prayer are alive, growing, and vibrant—things are cooking for Jesus!

I found some churches that made prayer a priority, and God is making these churches His priority. They have not let the business of having church rob them of the joy of prayer. Their "I, me, my, and mine" philosophy has been replaced with a "He, Him, His, and *glory to God*" mind-set. And they are making a difference in the world!

I sat in a worship service when the pastor led the congregation in an extended time of prayer. As he continued to offer a lengthy prayer, I realized how deeply and sincerely he was praying. I began to see the effects in the congregation: people were kneeling by their seats, many came to the front of the church with their entire families, some were weeping (how long has it been since I have seen that?). It was a powerful time in the church, and at the same time, this senior pastor was teaching his flock how to pray as well as reinforcing the importance of prayer. If a church is too busy to pray—they are too busy!

A few churches had rooms set aside for prayer, and there were folks there praying during the service. How encouraging! One church has folks praying in the prayer room every minute the pastor is preaching. This happens every time someone is in the pulpit. This is the pastor's prayer team, and a bunch of church members volunteer for it and share in this joyful work. They are a strong and growing church, filled with spiritual excitement. I wonder why.

I also visited churches that had no evidence of a prayer ministry—not only no physical indications but no spiritual evidence either. When there was prayer during the worship service, most prayers were very brief. Some seemed mechanical, and some were read, sung, or chanted in a monotone voice.

I did a little review of the church bulletins collected during my church visits. A few churches have no bulletins, and a large number of others do not print an order of service in their bulletin. From the bulletins printed with an order of service, I randomly selected fifty to see if prayer was listed. I found twenty-three references to prayer. Most included a designated type of prayer, such as "Prayer of—," as follows:

- There were prayers of confession, praise offering, the people, preparation for worship, the church, invocation, adoration, thanksgiving, supplication, illumination, assurance, forgiveness, pardon, common concerns, the day, and praise.
- Other printed descriptions were personal prayer, the Lord's Prayer, silent prayer, offertory prayer, Eucharistic prayer number 1, and invocation.

It seems, unfortunately, that the only time some people pray is when they attend church. Yes, it is better than nothing, but it is certainly a feeble way to demonstrate to God love for Him, let alone faith and trust and desire for His activity in personal lives.

Why don't churches spend more time in prayer? Charles Spurgeon said, "A church or person that is lukewarm is practicing the worst form of blasphemy!" Perhaps that's it—a lukewarm church avoids prayer. Jesus called the church at Laodicea lukewarm, and we all know what He said about them: "I will spit you out of My mouth" (Revelation 3:16). The word translated *spit* literally means "vomit"! Not a pretty picture! Before God can do a work *through* a church, He must do a work *to* a church. This often starts with prayer and is accomplished through prayer.

Do people attend church looking forward to the corporate prayer time? Is it merely a formality with no real connection with God? Do they ever anticipate something great is going to occur when they pray? Why or why not?

A CHURCH THAT PRAYS VS. A CHURCH DEDICATED TO PRAYER

If asked, most church people would say, "Of course, we pray!" There is a huge difference between a church that "prays" and a church that is *dedicated* to prayer. Consider these definitions:

A church that prays, prays about what happens.
A church *dedicated* to prayer does things by prayer.

Note the differences:

Prays = fits prayer in
Dedicated = makes prayer a priority

Prays = prays when there are problems
Dedicated = prays when there are opportunities

Prays = announces prayer meeting, and some in the church show up
Dedicated = announces a prayer meeting, and the church shows up

Prays = asks God to bless what they are doing
Dedicated = asks God to enable it to do what He is blessing

Prays = frustrated by money shortfalls and backs down from projects
Dedicated = challenged by money shortfalls, calls for prayer, fasting, and faith

Prays = is tired, weary, and stressed out
Dedicated = mounts up on wings like eagles, runs, and doesn't grow weary

Prays = does things within its means
Dedicated = does things beyond its means as God leads

Prays = sees its members as its mission field
Dedicated = sees the world as its mission field

Prays = involved in the work of man
Dedicated = involved in the work of God

Which type of church do you think would be more effective?

Every church develops their own reputation about who and what they are. When referring to a church, have you ever heard people say the following:

- "That church is really mission minded."
- "They have a wonderful outreach to the homeless."
- "Their VBS is great every year!"
- "Every teenager in the community wants to attend their summer camps."
- "That church is known for evangelism—they baptized over five hundred people last year."

How many times have you heard this? "That is the most prayerful church I have ever seen!" If you've heard it at all, that's more often than I have.

The following are some statements about *prayer* that I have come up with based on the following:

1. Pastoral experiences during fifty years of full-time ministry
2. Serving as pastor of prayer in three different churches for twenty plus years
3. Visiting 115 churches and seeing firsthand their emphasis or lack of emphasis on prayer

Some of the statements are self-explanatory in and of themselves. Others will find elaboration in the remainder of the chapter.

- Prayer is the most powerful ministry in a church.

  o No prayer, no power—no power, no prayer!

- People spend time with who and what they love.

  o Your calendar and checkbook prove it!

- Two hundred people will show up for a barbecue but only a handful for a prayer meeting.

  o Priorities revealed!

- People learn to pray by practicing.

  o Just do it!

- Prayer is hard work, and it is never over.

  o Still breathing? Keep praying! Never give up!

- Everyone in the church can pray.

  o No special skills needed!

- The prayer life of a church is a reflection of the prayer lives of the pastor and staff.

  o   Influence trickles down!

- If you are not praying, there is something wrong with your faith.

  o   Read James 5:16 (hint: "Prayer...can accomplish much")!

- Real men lead on their knees.

  o   So do real churches!

- Snuggle up to God in prayer, and He will snuggle up to you.

  o   You'll be glad you did!

- A person who prays not at all—ever—needs to be saved.

  o   Your first prayer: *Forgive my sins and save me, Lord!*

Show me your calendar and your checkbook, and I will show you where your heart is and what you love most. Look at mine, and the same results will be ascertained. Remember the story of Nancy C.? I wanted to spend time with her, so I tried to arrange it.

When you were married, after the wedding ceremony, did you shake hands with your new spouse and say, "What a great wedding, I really enjoyed it! I will call you, and maybe we can have lunch next week." Of course not! Because of your love for each other, you wanted to spend time together and enjoy the intimate relationship of a married couple. It was your love that motivated your desire to be together. We all want to spend time with who and what we dearly love. The same scenario can be compared to our relationship with Jesus Christ.

In a prayer class I taught, I asked this hypothetical question, "If I said to you, 'If you will read your Bible for thirty minutes every day and pray for thirty minutes every day for one week without missing a day, I will give you $10,000 cash—would you do it?" I asked for a show of hands. Everyone in the room raised their hand. I then said, "So the question is not whether you *could* do it or not but how badly do you *want* to do it!" The room was silent and still!

Look at a list of regular activities or at a church calendar of events to see what they love most—how do they spend their time? Where is time spent with Jesus? If we asked Jesus how much He loved us, He would spread His arms to show us, and that was when He was nailed to the cross. How much love is that? The depth and breadth of His love for us is absolutely unfathomable! Doesn't it just make sense that someone who loves us that much deserves being loved? That's what prayer is—loving on God!

I have attended, participated in, and led scores of Christian seminars, retreats, workshops, and conferences on the local, state, and national stage. As an attendee, I would review the list of courses offered and always signed up for every prayer course. A recurring trend at these events was this: a breakout room dealing with "Stress in the Ministry" would be packed and overflowing while the room where the topic was prayer had plenty of empty seats. I wonder if there was a connection? I think so—correction, I know so!

Maybe we need to step back and put prayer in perspective. The Almighty, All-Powerful Creator God and Sovereign of the universe invites us to come into His presence to talk with Him. Can anyone actually fathom that thought? Staggering, isn't it! Not only does He invite us, but He encourages us to do so—He even desires our fellowship! And not only does He wish to hear from us, but He makes it a two-way conversation. If that is not precious enough, He wants us to bring the burdens of our heart, the needs of our life, our worries and cares, our requests—and He will answer. There's even more, of course. That's just a brief reminder to jog our senses about prayer.

So out of His incredible love, God has provided this very special privilege—prayer. And this gift is available to all His children. No particular talents or abilities are required. You might not be able to sing in the choir, go on mission trips, play an instrument in the praise band or orchestra, or teach a Bible class. But everyone in the church can pray. From 3-year-old toddlers to 103-year-old toddlers, everyone can pray! No one is excluded!

Since everyone can participate in prayer, it should be promoted at every age level. When children pray, "Thank you God for mommy and daddy and my dog," the angels surely sing because the prayer is coming straight from their innocent hearts. God desires our communication with Him. He wants to hear from us. No special language is required if we just speak with sincerity from our heart.

I have two grandchildren, Ty and Tatum. I was there when they were born—Ty in 1997, and Tatum in 2006. I remember when they first made cute little baby cooing sounds. Then came some other goofy noises and a few jumbled words. Grandkids are cute and fun when they are learning to talk. We listen intently and encourage their attempts at verbal communication. We are thrilled when they babble a word or two and begin to make a little sense. Oh, how we love our grandkids! If you think our love is deep and wide for our grandkids, just think how much our Heavenly Father loves us! He is equally eager to hear even a few stumbling words from His children!

When my daughter, Amy, was a small child, she would say "wam" for water and "gunk" if she wanted a drink. In the late evening, Ty would say, "It's darking outside"—which, translated, meant, "It is getting dark." That kind of stuff makes for wonderful stories. It's cute when the kids are little. But if they continued to speak like that when they are grown, it would be embarrassing—actually a real tragedy! What a shame it would be if my adult daughter, mother of two, still said "gunk" today instead of drink! Why don't they still talk baby talk? They have grown and matured. They have gained knowledge. They have practiced talking. Their speech has developed in keeping with their physical development.

How do you think our Lord feels when those who have been His children for years don't really know how to talk to Him? It is an even greater tragedy! We have the ability to go right into the presence of God to make our requests known, and many churches and individuals are still praying like a toddler.

Individuals and churches learn to pray by praying. Prayer needs practice. The more practice, the more adept we become. I'll even take it a step further. All of us have heard the phrase, "Practice makes perfect." I don't buy that—*perfect* practice makes perfect! One of the most difficult challenges I have while teaching young folks to play banjo, guitar, and ukulele is this: some come to me knowing how to play a little bit but have learned the incorrect technique. Now it is hampering their progress and holding them back from advancing further. They have been practicing incorrectly and now must relearn, which can be difficult.

The same is true with praying. Some folks have been praying the same way, reciting the same prayer words over and over for years. Their boring and monotonous prayers have become meaningless to them—I wonder if their prayers even affect God the same way! It may be time to take a step forward to improve the quality of their prayer time.

> When I was a child, I used to speak like a child, think like a child, reason like a child; when I became a man, I did away with childish things. (1 Corinthians 13:11, NASB)

There is nothing wrong with reading a book on prayer or attending a prayer seminar. The more you learn about prayer, the better. But there are no shortcuts to prayer. It takes time and effort and more time and more effort. Here is the real blessing. The more time you spend in prayer, the more time you want to be with our Lord—and the reverse is also true.

When I retired and began to clear out my office at the church, I had what you could call a modest library. Over the years, I had gathered a collection of several hundred books, covering a wide range of topics. Some were very important to me while others I had never even opened, much less read. I went through all of them and gave 90 percent to the church library. Of the ones I chose to keep, over half were written about prayer. There are dozens of excellent books on the Christian market today that can be a wonderful source of help in the area of prayer. Being in prayer ministry, I was always looking for all the help I could get. Reading books on prayer has greatly enlarged my perspective and helped me tremendously in my personal prayer experience. The subject of prayer is still a major focus of my life and probably always will be.

Hand Me Another Brick is the title of a book by Chuck Swindoll that was published in February 1983. It recounts the story of Nehemiah and his quest to rebuild the wall around Jerusalem—which, from a human perspective, was totally impossible. No matter what was going on, Nehemiah would just say, "Hand me another brick"; and with God as the CEO and Master Builder, the wall was finished in fifty-two days. This book was a wonderful influence in my life when I was facing my own personal wall. Nehemiah's victory and my victory came as an answer to the prayers we each prayed. No doubt about it! Without prayer, Nehemiah could not have finished the wall; and without prayer, I could not have torn down my personal wall.

Max Lucado is one of my favorite authors. God has gifted him with a special way with words, and his writings have influenced my Christian walk. In one of his recent books, published by Thomas Nelson, titled *Before Amen: The Power of a Simple Prayer*, chapter 8 (page 100), he says,

> Prayer! Since God works, prayer works. Since God is good, prayer is good. Since you matter to God, your prayers matter in Heaven. You're never without hope, because you are never without prayer. And on the occasions you can't find words to say, pull these out of your pocket:
> FATHER, YOU ARE GOOD. I NEED HELP. HEAL ME. THANK YOU, IN JESUS' NAME, AMEN.

This not only applies to individuals but to churches as well. Our walk with our Lord—the every-minute, every-hour and everyday challenges we face as individuals and churches need to be approached first and foremost with prayer.

THE EXEMPLARY PRAYER LIFE OF JESUS

Since the disciples said to Jesus, "Teach us to pray" (Luke 11:1), there must be something to it. I can't help but think they were prompted to make this request because they had observed His prayer life and recognized its effects. You will notice they did not ask Him to teach them how to preach, lead singing, or organize a small group ministry, or anything else. They simply said, "Teach us to pray."

I have never found anyone in the Christian community who claims prayer is not important or that it is not vital to victorious living for the individual and for the church at large. What an individual and church are on their knees is really what they are.

The forty books I have on the subject of prayer focus on the various aspects and characteristics of prayer, ranging from "what is prayer?" to "how to pray." A lot of time, energy, research, and prayer were all part of each author's efforts. Although I have gained numerous insights on prayer, which have enriched my prayer experience and helped me with church prayer ministry, nothing compares with studying the prayer life of Jesus Christ.

Jesus's prayers were focused, intense, real, powerful, and effective. A church's prayers should have the same characteristics. I love the fact that Jesus is entirely God and entirely man at the same time, so His prayers were heavenly and human at the same time. His human life was a life of prayer. Prayer was not something Jesus used here and there but was what He was and is. Prayer to Jesus was like breathing is to us. It is a life-sustaining essential. His prayer life was directly proportional to the power He displayed and the love He embodied.

He prayed all the time because He had to pray all the time. He prayed when He was standing (Matthew 14:19), kneeling (Luke 22:41), and in Matthew 26:39, He "fell on His face" to pray. The church should follow His example. Jesus also shut Himself in with God in private prayer and shut the world out as He prayed in secret (Matthew 6:6). He also prayed in public with others. His longest prayer was when He was with His disciples in John 17. He prayed in the morning (Mark 1:35), in the evening (Mark 6:46), and He spent the night in prayer (Luke 6:12–13). Jesus prayed often and a lot, and so should we as individuals, and so should the church as a collective body.

These were some of the times when Jesus prayed:

- When He faced a crisis (Luke 9:18)
- When He performed miracles (Matthew 15:36, John 11:41–42, and Mark 9:14)
- When He finished a great work (Matthew 14:23)
- When He was under great pressure and stress (Mark 1:35 and Luke 4:42)
- When He was filled with great sorrow (John 6:15)
- When He was dying (Luke 23:46)

And He is still praying for us today!

Jesus's prayer life is the perfect example for us. Words referring to prayer like *petition, supplication, thanksgiving, adoration, praise,* and *perfect submission* to his Father are indicated in His prayers (Luke 22:42). Read and study Jesus's prayers, and you will find one aspect of prayer missing. Confession of sins and asking for forgiveness are absent. Jesus was perfect and holy; therefore, there were no sins in His life to confess and ask forgiveness for. Jesus is the ultimate prayer warrior. The apostle Paul in 1 Thessalonians 5:17 commanded us to "pray without ceasing." That command applies to the church today.

Whether you believe it or not, that youth camp you volunteered for as a cabin sponsor will eventually be over. Vacation Bible School, choir practice, and even the pastor's in-depth Wednesday night study of the Revelation will eventually end. Prayer never ends. You never get to the end of it. It is not a six-week course or a thirteen-week study but a lifetime of commitment and hard but rewarding work.

I recently was asked to visit a large church to assist and advise them about a very serious and challenging situation. I met with the pastor and sixteen of the deacons, elders, and other leadership. I knew that the only way this church was going to get out of this crisis was for our Lord to take the twenty-two men in that room by the hand and lead them through it. I could sense a heavy burden as I walked into the room. I knew everyone else was feeling the extreme pressure and hurt that this ungodly situation had created.

We met at 7:00 p.m., and I told them, "Before we even begin this meeting, let's pray and ask our Lord to intervene in this situation and to lead, guide, and direct us." We were sitting at a series of tables in the shape of a rectangle. I turned to the man on my left and said, "You start our prayer time, and we will go around the table, and I will close." I glanced up at a large clock on the wall, and it was 7:04 p.m. when our prayer time began. We prayed around the tables. As the last man was praying, I glanced at the clock, and it was now 7:27 p.m. What? It took twenty-three minutes for twenty-two men to pray about the most serious situation in the church? When the last man said amen, I did not pray. Instead, I simply stated, "We are going to pray around the table again. God means business, and so should we."

No prayer, no power! A church must continually promote and focus on prayer. Prayer will eventually become a powerful habit, the people will become holy, God will show up—then just hang on and watch what happens. Don't worry, you won't overshoot heaven, but you might think you will.

Remember that good reputation a church can gain because of something they do in an outstanding manner? Do you long for folks to drive by your church and say, "That church is the most prayerful church!"? What could you do about it? Here's something that certainly caught the attention of the community.

At one of the churches I served, we started a ministry called Drive-Thru Prayer. That's right! Our church was located on a very busy freeway where more than one hundred thousand cars pass by every day. There is a long stretch of feeder road between the freeway and the church property. On Thursday evenings, as you drive along the feeder, you will see more than fifty signs along the curb that read, "Drive-Thru Prayer" or "Need Prayer? Drive on in!"—all with arrows pointing to a parking-lot entrance.

When people drive in, there are signs directing them to a nearby parking lot. With a tent as their base, trained and dedicated prayer warriors are ready to walk up to the car, introduce themselves, and ask, "What can I pray with you about?" This is a great ministry! Countless numbers of people have driven in with specific requests and have been met with loving concern and prayers offered to the One who has all the answers. There is no other agenda. Drivers do not register their names and contact info or ask questions beyond the request for prayer. Not only is this a powerful ministry to the community, but it provides an opportunity for volunteers to step out in faith and lead folks in prayer.

There are many victory-in-Jesus stories I could share. Here is just one that went far beyond the pray-with-you-for-your-need scenario. A man drove in, was greeted, and asked the question, "What can I pray with you about?" The man responded, "I don't know how to pray." After a brief conversation, and sensing the openness of the driver, the volunteer shared the plan of salvation, and this man surrendered his life to Christ right there in his car! Then he asked, "Are you going to be here for a while? I want to go get my wife." He did, and she accepted Christ too! Both were baptized a while later to give public testimony of their salvation experience, and today they are active members in the church. Many people have been brought closer to the Lord as they have been prayed for in their time of need. But in this case, God brought a double blessing!

Like many other things, the tendency toward a strong prayer focus in a church always comes from the top. It flows from the hearts of the pastors and staff members. If a church doesn't have some type of prayer ministry or sustained prayer effort, it is likely that the pastor and staff don't either. If prayer is vital in a personal way to the leadership, they will make sure the same is true for the congregation.

Prayer won't just happen. Church leaders need to step forward and emphasize and promote prayer in the church. How many churches do you know that have a minister of prayer? How about a strong prayer ministry?

Praise God, I have never served in a church that did not have some real prayer warriors. Just start a prayer ministry, and those will be the first to come. Sometimes they are the folks you would not expect, but under their kind and quiet demeanor is a giant of a Christian prayer warrior. Just look at their spiritual armor, and you can tell they have been to hell and back. You will notice that their armor is bloodstained, dented, scraped, and battle-worn. You don't have to do much training with them. They have been on the front lines of spiritual battles for a long time. These folks are dedicated, strong, and godly.

Warning: Satan *hates* prayer. He might not get too upset about other programs at the church. But start making prayer a priority and seriously praying and get ready for a fight! But don't let that scare you—we are on the winning side, you know. Satan is already a defeated foe!

Here are a few thought-provoking statements written by some spiritual giants of the faith who were, first and foremost, prayer warriors. There are many others that could be quoted. I ask you to please read and meditate on these—may they sink deeply into your soul and stir you to fall on your knees!

- "What a man is, he is alone on his knees before God, and no more" (Robert Murray McCheyne).

- "The greatest thing anyone can do for God and man is pray. It is not the only thing; but the chief thing. The great people of the earth today are the people who pray. I do not mean those who talk about prayer; nor those who say they believe in prayer; nor yet those who can explain about prayer: but I mean those people who take time to pray" (S. D. Gordon).
- "The one concern of the devil is to keep Christians from praying. He fears nothing from prayer-less studies, prayer-less work, and prayer-less religion. He laughs at our toil, mocks at our wisdom, but trembles when we pray" (Samuel Chadwick).
- "Prayer is the channel through which all good flows to man. Prayer is a privilege, a sacred, princely privilege. Prayer is a duty, an obligation most binding and most imperative, which should hold us to it. But prayer is more than a privilege, more than duty. It is the appointed condition of getting God's aid. It is the venue through which God supplies man's wants" (E. M. Bounds).
- "Prayer is the single most powerful weapon in the universe. It can be launched from a spot no larger than a place to kneel, travel at the speed of thought, hit any target in the universe, and there is absolutely no defense against it" (Jack Taylor).
- "Prayer is the energy that enables the Christian soldier to wear the armor and wield the sword" (Warren Wiersbe).
- "Prayer is work. Prayer is no game…prayer is the opposite of leisure. It's something to be engaged in, not indulged in. It's a job you have to give priority to" (Elisabeth Elliott).
- "When we work, we work; but when we pray, God works!" (Unknown).

TO CONCLUDE

No prayer, no power; and no power, no prayer. It is that simple. Prayer is always in vogue—it's never out of date. I have seen a resurgence of prayer in many churches, and the absence of prayer in far too many others. It is especially encouraging to see pastors on their knees during worship services, leading the church in a pastoral prayer. The churches that are making an impact in their communities are praying churches. They pray individually and collectively. It is just a fact. Those that are really cooking are praying churches, and those that are dead in the water are not praying churches.

Don't be one to make feeble excuses about not having more prayer in your church. Churches have been anesthetized and lulled into doing nothing in this area. We seem to think that if we just teach folks to "lead good, clean Christian lives, smile, love everybody, attend church regularly, join a Bible study class, and give some money"—everything will be fine. Wrong!

Churches must be proactive in prayer. Every church must wholly depend on God, boldly proclaim the wonderful message of Jesus Christ from their pulpit, pray, and invite people to respond to the greatest message ever proclaimed—*Jesus saves!*

> The one who mobilizes the Christian church to pray will make the greatest contribution to world evangelization in history. (Andrew Murray)

Will you be the one?

11

Our Churches Need CPR! Christ-Produced Revival

In December 1891, at Springfield College in Boston, Massachusetts, Dr. James Naismith put the finishing touches on an assignment his athletic director, Dr. Luther Gulick, had given him. He had been asked to come up with some kind of physically demanding game that the football players could participate in during their off-season so they would stay in top physical condition through the entire year.

With a couple of large peach baskets, a soccer ball, and a ladder, a new game was invented—he named it *basketball*. Dr. Naismith nailed one basket on a wall at one end of the gym and the other on the opposite end, each ten feet from the floor. It worked. The players ran back and forth and all around the gym area, trying to throw the soccer ball in a peach basket.

Since they were running helter-skelter, Dr. Naismith painted lines on the floor in the shape of a large rectangle. The peach baskets were at the opposite ends of the form. When they moved on the court with the ball, they were required to bounce it on the floor with only one hand at a time to improve their hand-eye coordination. One of the players asked Dr. Naismith, "What do you call this part of the game?" The quick thinking doctor responded, "Dribbling."

The newly invented game was a success. The football team did a lot of running and had fun doing it. (The keeper of the ladder was in great shape too. His job was to place the ladder against the wall, climb up, and retrieve the ball from the peach baskets.)

A few years later, they replaced the peach baskets with metal rims, much to the relief of the ladder guy. The game enjoyed growing popularity, and on January 18, 1896, the first college basketball game was played. The score was 15–12 in a game between Chicago University and Iowa University respectively. The rest is history.

In the good old USA, the month of March is referred to as March Madness. Does that mean anything to you? I asked my wife that question, and she said it must be related to Washington politics! Wrong! March Madness refers to the nationwide NCAA college basketball tournament held from sea to shining sea and across our fruited plains every March. The dream of every university basketball team is to get to what is called the Big Dance. There are all kinds of conference tournaments and play-off games going on, coast-to-coast, all trying to qualify for the NCAA tourney. When all the conference play-offs are over, the NCAA committee will invite sixty-four teams to the Big Dance. The NCAA tournament is single elimination. Losers go home; winners advance. It looks like this:

- 64 teams are selected for the tournament
- 32 teams are left after the first round of play
- 16 are referred to as the sweet sixteen
- 8 are left from another round of play, which are called the elite eight
- 4 are left and called the final four

The winner of the final four becomes the NCAA basketball champion. Just a sidenote for all basketball purists: There are really sixty-eight teams selected for the tournament. Four are considered "play-in" games—it is too long and complicated to explain.

This is a *huge* media event. The NCAA team-selection process, the regional games, the brackets, the sports pages, and magazines are all about this tournament. It is truly March Madness. I love it! I played basketball, coached, and was a basketball official. The only injury I received during my dull, bench-sitting, unproductive college basketball career was when I fell off the ladder retrieving the ball from the peach basket! Insert smiley face here!

What would it look like if we made a sixty-four-item life tournament bracket? If we filled in sixty-four things that we really love and consider very important in our lives, what would the sixty-four be? Then we could take the sixty-four, play the first round of "life," and eliminate the list down to thirty-two. And we'll continue to repeat the process and go from thirty-two to sixteen, sixteen to eight, eight to four, and then two to one. What would be the number one thing in our lives? Although the list would vary from person to person, here's a sample list of sixty-four things that some would consider highly important in their life:

1. Fame	23. Security
2. Power	24. Wisdom
3. Friends	25. Automobiles
4. Social status	26. Peace
5. Sports	27. Jesus
6. Travel	28. Happiness
7. Fitness	29. Business
8. Sex	30. IRAs
9. Education	31. Politics
10. Wealth	32. Hunting
11. Work	33. Recognition
12. Prestige	34. Cattle
13. Clothes	35. Tranquility
14. Church	36. Affirmation
15. Success	37. Hobbies
16. Food	38. Diamonds
17. Youth	39. Parents
18. Beauty	40. Contentment
19. Skills	41. Fishing
20. Possessions	42. Spouse
21. Home	43. Social Status
22. Popularity	44. Children

45. Land	55. Intelligence
46. Bonds	56. Body Building
47. Grandkids	57. Investments
48. Marriage	58. Family
49. Partnerships	59. Reputation
50. Relationships	60. Ranch
51. Bank accounts	61. Airplanes
52. Stocks	62. Drugs
53. Music	63. Alcohol
54. Bible	64. Gold

Some of the sixty-four things listed are not necessarily good or bad. That verdict might be based on how much time, energy, and emphasis an individual might invest in them and what they would have to eliminate from their lives to obtain it.

I have seen people dedicate their entire lives to pursuing some of these things. Countless counseling sessions from over fifty years in the ministry have revealed to me the tragedy of lives wasted by men chasing the wind. It's all about what you treasure, what you value the most above all else.

In the first round of the sixty-four-item life bracket, going from 64 to 32 is not that difficult. Sure you have to think a bit, but what about going from 32 to 16? Tough decisions abound when you get to the elite eight and definitely the final four. Your actions and choices will be a direct reflection of what you care about, what you love the most, and your priorities in life.

I wonder what the life bracket of a church would look like? If you got the membership of one church in a large room, with all members together for a fill-in-the-bracket party, what would the bracket look like? Would it be very different from that of another denomination? What do you think the differences would be? What about the similarities?

When I was a teenage boy, I remember seeing people on their knees at the altar of my home church, weeping and praying for the lost. People were burdened for the unsaved of the community. I have wonderful recollections of people of all ages standing up in church, sharing testimonies about how they came to know Christ as their personal Savior and how their lives had been so dramatically changed they just had to let people know! From conversations with others of my generation, I know this was not uncommon among churches of that day. I can't help but think those churches had their brackets filled in correctly—their head official was Jesus Christ, the Commissioner of the league of life.

During my sixteen months as a secret church shopper, I found that such happenings in churches today are by far the exception rather than the rule. In fact, I am sad to report that what I experienced in church as a boy is practically nonexistent in today's churches.

In the process of writing this book, I visited with a bunch of my pastor friends asking for their advice and input. A common theme began to surface as many suggested or even urged that I include the need for revival—a fresh anointing of the Holy Spirit.

I have found this desire for revival within many circles of my acquaintance and know lots of people earnestly praying for revival. There is a definite connection between prayer and revival. Historically, every great revival of modern times has been preceded by a great movement of prayer. The subject of revival has been a major focus of prayer for my wife and me for at least twenty-five years. I am aware of groups of prayer warriors that meet together regularly for the specific purpose of beseeching God to send revival. As we see our country spiraling downward deeper and deeper into godlessness, there is more and more concern. Revival is our only hope. We desperately need CPR—Christ-produced revival!

Does the word *revival* sound old-fashioned and out of date? It is not a term that we hear frequently. Often, when people today hear the word *revival*, they envision a big tent with a huge sign that reads REVIVAL hung between two towering poles, perhaps with another sign declaring, JESUS SAVES. Or a football stadium might come to mind, with a choir singing and someone preaching to a large crowd.

However, the true concept of revival is not an evangelistic campaign to win the lost to Christ. Hang with me here! That may well be the outcome of a revival, but a revival is to revive Christians—those who have already been born again into the family of God. Those who across denominational lines are true believers, making up the body of Christ, sometimes called the universal church. When the church is revived, God can work through those revived individuals and congregations to lead the lost to salvation in Christ.

People who have never accepted God's salvation by faith in Jesus Christ are spiritually dead. Dead people cannot be revived—they need life! All of us were born spiritually dead. Jesus said, "I am the resurrection and the *life*" (John 11:25, NASB). And again, He said, "I am the way, and the truth, and the *life*; no one comes to the Father but through Me" (John 14:6, NASB). When we trust Christ as Savior and Lord, we become spiritually alive because we receive the life of Christ.

I feel the greatest need in churches today is not new buildings, more ministries, or more mission trips. The greatest need in our churches today is for those who call themselves Christians to fall on their faces in prayer, be revived, be living proof of Christ's life within, and daily live out their faith. When this happens, all other ministries of the church will be positively affected. Let me make this very clear—the single greatest need in our churches is for Christians to get close to Jesus Christ and live, act, talk, and walk in His way! When God's people do this, a lost world will take notice. When they see Christlikeness in us, they will get a glimpse of Jesus. When believers are revived, Jesus will be glorified, and all men will be drawn to Him.

We all remember the tragic incident that took place a decade or so ago in a Pennsylvania Amish community. A young man walked into a one-room schoolhouse, shot ten female students (five of whom died), and then committed suicide. For no apparent reason, certainly with no provocation, an individual wreaked havoc on a community of quiet, peace-loving, godly people.

How did they react? Their grief was apparent, of course. But they reached out in love and sympathy to the family of the shooter. They spoke of forgiveness toward the one who had committed this horrific wrong. In short, the Amish people reflected the character of Jesus, and the world took notice. The worldly news media, typically prone to suppress expressions of Christianity, were compelled to take a second look and print stories about the remarkable response of the Amish.

A similar incident has taken place more recently. A young man attended a Bible study in a historic church in Charleston, South Carolina. He was welcomed by the members and joined with them in listening to an hour-long Bible lesson. Then, for no apparent reason, the man took out a gun and shot and killed nine of the members, including the pastor, before taking his own life. Again, a group of Christian people, greatly wronged by this unspeakable atrocity and deeply grieving, did not respond in anger or resentment but with a loving and forgiving attitude. Once more, the country was amazed, and media reports made comment on the unusual and commendable Christian behavior of the church members. A well-known national commentator remarked about having never seen a more profound demonstration of grace and forgiveness.

The two stories exemplify the impact of Christlike character on our non-Christian culture. What if all Christian people displayed godliness to such a degree that it was apparent to all? How much more effective could we be if the world could see in our behavior and demeanor and lifestyle the life of Jesus personified? Too often, Christian people just blend in with the rest of the population. There seems to be little or no distinction between believers and nonbelievers. A genuine revival among Christ's church that would bring about radical life change would make a huge impact in our world! Jesus said in John 12:32, speaking of His crucifixion to come, "And I, if I am lifted up from the earth, will draw all men to

Myself." If we as the church would consistently showcase the life of Christ in us, it would surely attract outsiders to Him! Oh, how I long to see that happen!

During my church visits, I found myself wondering if some churches were just completely dead even though they continued having services week after week. I began to see the truth of estimates I have heard—that perhaps 80 percent of people across the board in local churches today are not truly saved. They are Christian in name only, professing to be believers but having no life within. In contrast, there were other churches so spiritually alive, healthy, and on fire for our Lord that I just enjoyed sitting there watching them kick Satan's butt! These churches are vibrant, growing, effective, and are having an impact in their communities. I know what their final bracket would look like!

Regrettably, the obviously alive churches are few and far between. It doesn't take that much research to gather information from denominational organizations about diminishing church-growth patterns, low number of conversions, lack of new church plants, and too many church closings and see that things are moving in the wrong direction. When you check spiritual vital signs, they are faint and weak. An elder in one church told me, "We are about two to three funerals away from closing our doors." In another mainline denominational church I visited, the auditorium had seven hundred seats, and there were only thirty-six people in attendance counting the three pastors and me. What? Do folks think God is dead or something? What do you think their life bracket would look like?

Decline is happening in many churches despite the fact there has never been more information available focusing on church growth, building a successful church, and other related topics. Churches seem to be in a spiritual rut and just can't turn the corner. By the way, I've heard a *rut* defined as just a "long grave without an end"—something to think about!

Some churches have spectacular six-flags-over-Jesus productions with lots of bling and glitz, presented in a show-business atmosphere. This often attracts large crowds. Some very large churches are founded on over-the-top services, programs, and activities that appeal to many. I am reminded of a quote by Charles Spurgeon: "Just because a church is big doesn't mean it is healthy—it could be just swollen!"

While I certainly favor the removal of barriers that keep people from church—and I would never purposely be offensive—I feel like some pastors/churches carry this to the extreme. The attitude of some church leadership is to never say or do anything that might make folks feel uncomfortable. It's an intentional strategy to make everybody feel good about themselves, keep up their spirits, dish out nothing but positive advice, and focus on how to be successful in life. Let's be happy, happy, happy! The problem is—that is not biblical.

The message of the gospel of Christ could be considered by some as very offensive. After all, people must be confronted with their sin. They must realize they have sinned against God and need forgiveness for their sin. Without acknowledging personal sinfulness, a person will not realize their need for the Savior and His forgiveness. People are lost and going to hell—they need to turn their backs on sin, turn their faces to God, repent, and receive Jesus Christ as their Lord and Savior. I don't get it! Let's get back to preaching the Word, praying, and eliminating worldly influences that have crept into our churches.

It seems to me that in the business of doing church, we have forgotten *Whose* we are and for *Whom* we are workers. Are we more concerned about the denomination or numbers than God? Do we cringe when the other church down the street has a full parking lot and we don't? Do you relish it when you hear a story about another church's conflicts? If individuals, churches, or denominations are afflicted with troubles and sorrows, are you amused and delighted about it? How do you react? What is your response? If it is anything short of prayer for those involved, we should be on our knees repenting and asking for forgiveness. We are not in competition with one another! We are players on the same team! We need to examine our life bracket. We need revival in our churches and in our personal lives.

What does it take to get a church healthy and, in some cases, raised from the dead? Only Jesus can raise the dead! If you want to know the ten basic steps for church growth, that is not what this is about. I want to share the three things you must have to be a success in anything—whether you are playing a sport, building a bench, taking cooking lessons, chasing a college degree, or learning to play a banjo. Whatever it is you set out to do, you must consider these three things: knowledge, skill, and passion. Here is an illustration of this principle.

You and your spouse have worked in the yard for weeks, making it beautiful and in order. You have endured heat, rain, blisters, mosquitoes, and have temporarily won the war over weeds and fire ants. The flowers you planted are blooming, the bushes are trimmed, the birdbath is level, the yard is fertilized, and it just looks great! Your wife has one more idea. She wants a decorative bench by the garage. She suggests, "Instead of spending a bunch of money on a bench, why don't you just build one!"

Are you as construction challenged as I am? The problem is, you don't know how to build a bench (knowledge). You have never built anything before. You have no tools and no experience (skills). And the main thing is you don't want to do it; you would hate every minute of it (passion). So instead, you run down to the local Lowe's and buy a $75 bench for $250. What was the real underlying problem? With enough passion for the project, you could have gained the knowledge (lots of self-help books out there). With a sincere passion, you could have acquired the tools and developed the skills to build the bench (practice would do wonders). But you didn't *want* to do it—no passion!

The point is that without passion for something, you won't get it done, whether it's building a bench or building a church or doing anything else. The amazing thing is that God provides all three things we need:

1. Knowledge. He has given us His Word, the Bible, the complete exhaustive instructions for everything in spiritual life.
2. Skills. He has given us the gifts of the Spirit, His Holy Spirit–empowered enablement to do the job.
3. Passion. He has given us a new heart, a love for Him, a desire to please Him.

Then how do we mess up? We follow our old ways. We allow distance to come between us and Him. We let sinful, selfish desires creep in. That's why we need to be revived. But when we as individuals or as a collective church body apply His Word to our lives, renounce our sins, and stay close to Him in humble submission to His will and way, He provides the power to "get 'er done," whatever the task may be!

In 1980, three outstanding college basketball players graduated from their respective universities. Each player's last name began with the letter *M*, so they were referred to as the M squad. Pete Maravich, Rick Mount, and Calvin Murphy were all-Americans in every sense of the word. All of them played proball in the NBA (National Basketball Association).

- Pete "Pistol Pete" Maravich wore number 44 on his uniform in the pros because that was his scoring average at LSU.
- Rick Mount had the greatest, most fluid jump shot. To practice, he shot ten thousand jump shots a week.
- Calvin Murphy played many successful years in the NBA and led the NBA in free-throw percentage.

The one common denominator among the M squad was their *passion* for the game—a passion that consumed their lives.

Pete Maravich is a most interesting character. Although he had an outstanding NBA career, he had a troubling life. His fame and fortune led him down a road of drugs, alcohol, and near-fatal self-destruction. In his ten-year career, he achieved every basketball award possible. He was 6'5" and weighed 197 pounds and possessed talents beyond imagination. A leg injury forced him to retire from the NBA in 1980. Following retirement, he became a recluse for two years. During that period of time, Pete tried many religions and other pursuits to find peace with life after basketball.

Fortunately, his search led him to Jesus, the only source of true peace. He gave his life to Christ in 1982 and set out to use his basketball skills and reputation as a platform to tell others of what Jesus Christ had done in his life. On January 5, 1988, he was in California to record a program to be aired on *Focus on the Family*, a radio program hosted by Dr. James Dobson. The morning of the show, Pete and Dr. Dobson went to a nearby gym for a shootaround before the recording. Pete Maravich died on the court with a massive heart attack. The autopsy revealed that he had a rare heart condition that could have been fatal at anytime. In a 1984 interview, Pistol Pete had said, "I want to be remembered as a Christian, a person who serves Jesus to the utmost, not as a basketball player."

A church must have the passion to gain the knowledge and skills it takes to grow and maintain a vibrant, healthy, and exciting church. The big question is, How and where does a church get this type of passion?

Here is a list of *wrong* answers:

- Get a committee together to explore the possibilities.
- Attend a church-growth seminar.
- Visit growing churches.
- Bring in a denominational assessment team.
- Take a church survey.
- Schedule more ministries at your church.
- Start another service on Sunday mornings.

These are not bad things to do, but they are not the correct answers to the question about passion. However, they could possibly be some of the outcome of the passion the church generates. The following is an attempt to expand on earlier thoughts regarding passion, with more practical application in mind.

We can be thankful that we have all things through Christ. Even when we have wandered away from Him, He lovingly pursues us. It is through Him that we are able to be revived. He provides what we need—real power to become the light of the world and shake the gates of hell.

God provides the passion! How does a church obtain this? When the members of a church are totally sold out to God. A church must fall on their collective faces and pray, confess their sins, and live for Him 365 days 24-7. Often it begins at the top of the church and flows down to the congregation—pastor to staff, elders, deacons, volunteers, and the rest of the congregation. Love for Christ, obedience to His Word, and submission to His will put a church in a position to receive what they need most: a supernatural intervention of God! The church can be revived because God has invaded every person and every ministry.

A well-known Christian actor was in Houston having a Sunday evening dinner with a megachurch pastor and his family. The guest had been traveling across the USA, speaking in all types of churches. The pastor inquired as to his general thoughts of the churches where he had been. The actor responded by saying, "In your sermon this morning, you used the word *repent* several times. As I sat there listening, I realized that was the first time I had heard that word coming from a pulpit in the last year of my travels." There can be no revival without repentance of sin.

How likely is it that people will turn from their sinful ways when preachers are not even mentioning the subject? The answer is clear—you will not see this unless the penetrating, convicting, life-changing Word of God is being presented from the pulpit. It is the role of the Holy Spirit to apply the Word of God to the hearts of individuals to bring about the realization of sin and move the guilty one to repentance. To fail to preach repentance is to squelch the Holy Spirit's work in the lives of those who need to repent.

Why are churches sick, weak, and dying? Because Jesus is not running the show. He has been squeezed out of the church schedule because the church is too busy *doing church*. The energy, vitality, and strength that come from Jesus being in charge produces a loving, vibrant, effective church. This is not taught—it is caught. Simply stated, our churches need revival!

Some churches have become quite adept at using their technology, methodology, or entertainment capabilities to increase attendance numbers. The question is, What do they offer folks when they get there? Is God's Word being preached? Is the whole counsel of God the message presented? If not, the attendees are no better off than if they went to a movie or read a newspaper to solve their problems.

The *inflow* of God's Word into a church produces an *overflow* of His love, goodness, and mercy, which in turn becomes an *outflow* to others. The passion seen and demonstrated by the church, because of Christ's presence in their lives, is what points people to Jesus and draws them to church.

In the December 2014 issue of *Decision Magazine*, Jim Cymbala has an article titled "Real Power, Real Growth." He stated, "We [churches] owe them [those who attend] the unadulterated, powerful, life-giving Word of God, expressed in love and compassion, and not a diluted, imitation gospel that is powerless." The big question to churches is, What type of gospel is being presented? Is it the powerful, life-giving Word of God or a diluted and powerless imitation gospel message?

It is a matter of choice on the part of the individual church. This largely falls on the shoulders of the pastor. What do they choose to present? Are they going to lift the name of Jesus high, preach *from* the Bible rather than *about* it, offer opportunities for people to accept Christ as personal Lord and Savior, pray, and reach out to their community with the love of Christ? Or are they going to continue to follow traditions, remain spiritually lifeless, and stagnate in the same dull church box? Remember, it is a choice a church will make. The skill, knowledge, and passion come from Christ. When your church is all about Him, He provides the inflow of power and blessings that generates the overflow of His love that outflows on your community and changes everything. Nothing stays the same when Jesus shows up.

After sitting through 115 church services, I have seen the presence and, at times, the absence of Christ among all denominations. Christ loves His church and died for it. The more Christ's love is present in the lives of His children, the more passion is generated that enables God's power to flow in the family of God.

According to an information letter sent out recently from Franklin Graham and the Billy Graham Evangelistic Association, Vanuatu is one of the poorest island nations in the South Pacific. The first missionaries to serve on Vanuatu were killed by cannibals. When John G. Paton of Scotland was called by God to this island as a missionary, an elderly friend of his named Dickson warned him, "You will be eaten by cannibals!" Paton's response was astounding and priceless. His words could only be motivated by a deep love for Christ and His cause. Paton said,

> Mr. Dickson, you are advanced in years now and your own prospect is soon to be laid in the grave, there to be eaten by worms. I confess to you, that if I can but live and die serving and honoring the Lord Jesus, it will make no difference to me whether I am eaten by cannibals or by worms, and in the Great Day my resurrection body will rise as fair as yours in the likeness of our risen Redeemer.

Mr. Paton's words evidence a natural outflow of God's great love that resides in a man who allowed God to not only have residence in him but to control every part of his life. That is what the believer's life should be. God rewarded Paton's faithfulness, and he eventually saw thousands of people repent of their sins and accept Christ as their Lord and Savior.

This is not a Methodist, Church of Christ, Presbyterian, Lutheran, Baptist, or any other denominational thing—it is a family-of-God thing! It is Christ's church, and He wants it to be healthy and alive. He has a plan to make it happen, plenty of passion for us; and He gave us the Bible, an instruction book, that tells us what to do and how to get it done. Churches must do the following:

1. Have a pastor who lives and preaches the Word of God.
2. Fall on our collective faces and pray, seek God, and repent of sins.
3. Seek His will—not ours.
4. Follow His teachings, not what we think or what our denomination tells us, but what the Bible instructs.
5. Love everyone, even if they are not like us—they are God's creation. By the way, it is impossible to love different folks if we do not love God first.
6. Pray, listen to God, and follow His instructions.
7. Let our Lord build His church—we are just here to be His vehicle.
8. Praise His name, become Christ-centered, and Christ-controlled, not denomination-centered or tradition-centered.
9. Share the greatest news ever: *Jesus saves!*
10. Demonstrate by our actions: love, kindness, respect, forgiveness, patience all characteristics of God.

Revival comes from God—it is a supernatural thing! We cannot create it ourselves!

When it comes, enjoy the revival!

I admire the stance of one megachurch pastor I know. He invited other pastors of all denominations in the city, as well as leaders of parachurch ministries, to join him in praying for our city and our nation—for revival in the church. About sixty to eighty pastors accepted his invitation. They have intentionally arranged their schedules to make this a priority and have been meeting together once a month for over a year. Revival is on their hearts. My, how we need other pastors to take the lead in initiating prayer for revival!

The answer to the dwindling, declining, and dying church is the same answer that has always been—Jesus Christ! He is our Lord and Savior! He fills us with His abounding love, which enables us to proclaim the saving and life-changing gospel of Jesus Christ to everyone, everywhere, at all times. Victory in Jesus is assured. When individuals get right with God, our families will get right with God, and so will our churches. This will result in lost people being drawn to Christ and receiving Him as Lord and Savior. That is God's plan. To God be the glory!

Most followers of Christ are familiar with the story of the man who was lame from birth and spent his days at the pool of Bethesda, which is recorded in John 5:1–11. For thirty-eight years he lay there, helpless, crippled, and filthy. He knew the legend about the healing waters of the Bethesda pool. When the waters moved, the first one in the pool would be healed. However, because of his deformed and diseased body, he could not make it to the pool.

Jesus saw the man and had compassion for him. Notice what Jesus asked the man: "Do you want to be whole?" Jesus didn't say, "Do you want your legs healed?" And Jesus healed him. We as crippled churches and individuals must want to be *whole*! The more whole the human body is, the better life it affords. Strength, endurance, longevity are all characteristics of a whole human body. The same is true in the spiritual realm with the body of Christ—the church. When church members are whole, the church is whole.

There might be someone reading this who has never made a personal commitment to Jesus Christ. Please understand you are not saved by being a member of a church, regardless of the denomination; and you are not saved by being a good person or living a good life. Accepting Christ is a one-on-one, face-to-face encounter with Jesus. Here is what you need to know to make that life-changing decision for Christ.

Steps to Peace with God

Step 1

Why don't most people have this peace and abundant life that God planned for us to have? God loves you and wants you to experience peace and life. The Bible says,

> We have peace with God through our Lord Jesus Christ. (Romans 5:1)

> For God so loved the world that He gave His one and only Son, that whoever believes in Him shall not perish but have eternal life. (John 3:16)

> I have come that they may have life, and that they may have it more abundantly. (John 10:10)

Step 2

God created us in His own image to have an abundant life. He did not make us robots to automatically love and obey Him. God gave us a will and freedom of choice. We chose to disobey God and go our own willful way. We still make this choice today. This results in separation from God. The Bible says,

> For all have sinned and fall short of the glory of God. (Romans 3:23)

> For the wages of sin is death, but the gift of God is eternal life in Christ Jesus our Lord. (Romans 6:23)

People have tried in many ways to bridge this gap between themselves and God. The Bible says,

> There is a way that seems right to a man, but in the end it leads to death. (Proverbs 14:12)

> But your iniquities have separated you from your God: Your sins have hidden His face from you, so that He will not hear. (Isaiah 59:2)

People try being good, do good works, work to become religious, try philosophy, and live moral lives—hoping this will be a bridge between them and God. No bridge reaches God, except one.

Step 3
God's bridge is the *cross*.

Jesus Christ died on the cross and rose from the grave. He paid the penalty for our sin and bridged the gap between God and people. The Bible says,

> For there is one God and one mediator between God and men, the man Christ Jesus. (1 Timothy 2:5)

> For Christ died for sins once for all, the righteous for the unrighteous, to bring you to God. (1 Peter 3:18)

> But God demonstrates His own love for us in this: While we were still sinners, Christ died for us. (Romans 5:8)

God has provided the only way. Each person must make a choice.

Step 4
Our response: receive Christ. We must trust Jesus Christ as Lord and Savior and receive Him by personal invitation. The Bible says,

> Here I am! I stand at the door and knock. If anyone hears my voice and opens the door, I will come in and eat with him, and he with Me. (Revelation 3:20)

> Yet to all who received Him, to those who believed in His name, He gave the right to become children of God. (John 1:12)

> That if you confess with your mouth "Jesus is Lord", and believe in your heart that God raised Him from the dead, you will be saved. (Romans 10:9)

Will you receive Jesus Christ right now? Here is how you can receive Christ:

1. Admit your need (I am a sinner).
2. Be willing to turn from your sins (repent).
3. Believe that Jesus Christ died for you on the cross and rose from the grave.
4. Through prayer, invite Jesus Christ to come in and control your life through the Holy Spirit (receive Him as Lord and Savior).

How to Pray

Dear Lord Jesus,

I know that I am a sinner and need Your forgiveness. I believe that You died for my sins. I want to turn from my sins. I now invite You to come into my heart and life. I want to trust and follow You as Lord and Savior. In Jesus's name, amen.

If you prayed this prayer, the Bible says, "Everyone who calls on the name of the Lord will be saved" (Romans 10:13). Did you sincerely ask Jesus Christ to come into your life? Where is He right now? What has He given you?

For it is by grace you have been saved, through faith—and this not from yourselves, it is the gift of God—not by works, so that no one can boast. (Ephesians 2:8–9)

He who has the Son has life; he who does not have the Son of God does not have life. I write these things to you who believe in the name of the Son of God so that you may know that you have eternal life. (1 John 5:12–13)

Receiving Christ, we are born into God's family through the supernatural work of the Holy Spirit who indwells every believer. This is called regeneration, or the *new birth*. This is just the beginning of a wonderful new life in Christ. To deepen this relationship, you should do the following:

1. Read your Bible every day to know Christ better.
2. Talk to God in prayer every day.
3. Tell others about Christ.
4. Worship, fellowship, and serve with other Christians in a church where Christ is preached.
5. As Christ's representative in a needy world, demonstrate your new life by your love and concern for others.

If you want further help in the decision you have made, write to

Steps To Peace With God
Billy Graham Evangelistic Association
1 Billy Graham Parkway
Charlotte, NC 28201-0001
Toll Free: 1-877-247-2426

If you made the life-changing decision to accept Jesus Christ, you are now my brother or sister in Christ. God is our Heavenly Father, so we are all kin. It is great to have you in the family of God!

There is a good chance we will never meet and share a cup of coffee on this earth. Let's make a deal to meet in heaven, where all our brothers and sisters in Christ will be. I know I will be able to find you. You will have a big smile on your face. If I don't find you first, you can locate me at the feet of Jesus. I plan on spending the first ten thousand years of eternity at His feet, just praising Him and saying *thanks*.

12

The Frog and the Church in the Pot

In 1990, Regal Press published a 235-page book by George Barna titled *The Frog in the Kettle*, with the subtitle *What Churches Need to Know About Life in the Year 2000*. The book gives insights into how individuals, churches, and other organizations gradually move into places or accept attitudes that are dangerous without actually realizing what is happening. Barna suggests that we as churches and individuals don't ordinarily dive right in to shaky situations. However, we often slowly wade into the shallow end of danger; and before we know it, we are in over our heads.

His book is based on the fable about the frog in the pot, which basically contends that if you throw a frog in a pot of boiling water, it will hop right out. But if you put that frog in a pot of water at room temperature and slowly warm it to the boiling point, the frog doesn't figure out what is going on until it is too late. The story is a metaphor used to describe how gradual changes eventually become detrimental without us being aware it's even happening. The results are boiled frog.

To examine this theory and assumption, please consider these provocative questions:

- Can this happen to a church?
- Can a church or denomination begin to compromise its belief on something and drift into trouble and error as it cooks in its own juices?

- Is it possible for a church to be so busy trying to get things done that they get boiled in the process?
- Have churches been floating on errors for so long they are no longer aware of the truth?
- Can churches be so enamored and distracted by the bubbles in the water that they are majoring on minors?
- Is it possible for churches and staff members/elders to become so weakened by the hot water they are in that they become insensitive to obvious threats, much less slowly changing trends?
- Is it true that if a church doesn't see change happening that it is very difficult to deal with the aftermath?

If we ever had the opportunity to become acquainted, it would probably not take you long to discern that I am not the sharpest knife in the drawer or the brightest light on the Christmas tree. When I was in middle school, I was never chosen first for the spelling-bee team, but I was always chosen first for the basketball team. I am not a physicist, historian, biologist, or rocket scientist. The physiological ecology of thermal relations of amphibians and reptiles is not my forte. However, I think I am blessed with what I call plain common sense. I do recognize when things are not going well. I learned a long time ago (and the Bible confirms this), that when God is taken out of anything, it begins to decline, weaken, spoil, and eventually die.

After 115 visits to churches of 28 denominations, I sometimes felt that the church and all the "frogs" in attendance (including me) were following a list of things to do in the worship service but never got to the heart of what we were there to receive. It seemed that whatever message the speaker was trying to deliver was being pushed to the bottom of the pot without affecting any of us frogs. I can vividly remember leaving churches and thinking, *What was that sermon all about? What was the point presented? What spiritual application was I supposed to hear?*

The problem in some church pots was not the number of frogs in the pot, nor even the gradually increasing water temperature. The problem was—there was no rescue attempt. All the frogs in the pot were being led by a seemingly confused head bullfrog. To put it plainly, the clear proclamation of the Word of God was missing.

Just listen to the news or read the newspapers, and it appears that everything in the world around us is out of control. Virtues like truth, honesty, morality, compassion, and selflessness are rarely seen. The whole world seems to be going down the drain. Goodness and godliness are frowned upon and downplayed while countercultural actions are accepted and rewarded. How do you think our churches, homes, schools, and government are faring? Are these pillars of society stronger or weaker, better or worse, than they were twenty to thirty years ago? Even ten years ago?

Our country was built on a rock-solid foundation of faith, integrity, honesty, equality, courage, and hard work. We have maintained our strength and received the blessings of God. The basic pillars of our great nation have been these positive and lasting institutions: church, home/marriage/family, public schools, and government. Let's examine these four pillars that are part of the basic foundation of the United States of America.

1. The Church
2. The Home/Marriage/Family
3. The Public Schools
4. The Government

The Church

Is the church a strong and powerful influence in our society today? Some churches will do whatever it takes to attract a crowd, even if it is contrary to biblical teachings. They will worship tradition or a denomination; and because they are sitting in a pot of hot water, they won't change. It seems that many churches have abandoned the core teachings of the Bible and, at the same time, allowed the world to invade their fellowship. Many will do nothing about it because they have become too enthralled, entertained, and distracted watching the bubbles rising from the bottom of the pot.

When I was a boy, we had to go to the grocery store on Saturdays to shop because everyone closed their stores on Sundays so their employees and families could attend church. As time passed, special laws—referred to as blue laws in Texas—were passed, which allowed certain stores to be open on Sundays. What about today? If you didn't know what day it was, you could not tell if it was a Sunday or Tuesday.

And get this! Once upon a time, when I was in school, it was a common practice for teachers to *not* give homework on Wednesdays because that was church night! Can you believe that? We're talking about midweek church-service attendance being so widespread among the masses that allowances were made for homework! Gone are the days!

Stores today like Chick-fil-A, Mardel, and Hobby Lobby—owned by Christians—are closed on Sundays. Chick-fil-A displays a sign explaining why they are closed on Sundays, and I greatly admire their bold stand. Can you believe they are criticized and berated because of their stance? Of course, you can—it's a sign of our times!

Do you see the church-in-the-pot similarities? Are the morals of our nation higher today than in the past? Where is the church in the political process? Does it have an overwhelming influence in the affairs of our nation? Watered-down theology, wimpy sermons, weak and ineffective churches are common. Is there more to be said? It hasn't always been this way, but when the church exists in hot water, the frogs lose their kick—the church has no more influence.

The Home/Marriage/Family

A recent article in the *Houston Chronicle* listed the total number of divorces in the Houston area. It stated that over 50 percent of the couples that get married will be filing for divorce within twenty-four months or less. The article also stated that there had been a decline in divorce in the last few years. That's good news! Not really. Why the decline? Are people standing true to their commitments and honoring their marriage vows and values? No, not at all. The divorce rate has declined because the marriage rate has declined; more and more couples are opting to live together without committing to marriage.

Just because "everyone is doing it" doesn't make it right. Homes, marriages, and families are falling apart everywhere, and we suffer the consequences in every phase and level of society. The real victims and tragedies of divorce and destroyed families are the children. So many boys and girls are the innocent victims of this national plague. We see them lonely, failing in school, living self-destructive lifestyles, and longing for some type of security.

Every boy and girl needs a loving relationship with loving parents. There is no substitute for this. It is a basic element for a healthy family. Every young boy, whether he realizes it or not, asks the question, "Do I have what it takes to be a man?" Ever hear a little boy say, "Watch me, Dad," before he throws a baseball? Every little girl, knowingly or unknowingly, asks the question, "Am I beautiful and worth fighting for?" For example, she twirls around in her new dress and says, "Look, Daddy, I'm a princess!"

In both cases, the child has a deep longing for affirmation from their father. How many children live in homes where there is no father? He may be totally absent from their lives through divorce or abandonment. Or he may be living in the home but emotionally detached or unengaged with the lives of his children or even abusive. Each of those scenarios is extremely damaging. If a child's need for paternal love and affirmation is not met by their father, they will seek it elsewhere for the rest of their lives—most often through destructive behaviors. Workaholism, promiscuity, homosexuality, gang involvement, alcohol and drug abuse are just some of the outcomes.

The newspaper article with divorce statistics also explained the need to change the wording on many government forms to reflect the changes occurring in the family structure. Printed on various documents, under the heading of "Family Status," most used to read (or a similar variation):

_ Married
_ Single
_ Divorced
_ Widow/Widower

Today's forms read: (or a similar variation)

_ Traditional family (one man and one woman)
_ Blended
_ Same sex
_ Living together
_ Single mom
_ Single dad
_ Extended
_ Other

Shortly before the long-anticipated Supreme Court ruling on same-sex marriage, this full-page ad appeared in the *USA Today* newspaper. On June 11, 2015, the headline of the ad read,

> We ask you not to force us to choose between the state and the Laws of God.

Here is the opening paragraph[1] of an open letter to the Supreme Court justices of the United States (emphasis mine):

---

1   The marriage pledge can be read in its entirety at http://www. defendmarriage.org. It offers a more detailed defense of marriage and further expresses our unified resolve. Tens of thousands of very concerned Americans have signed the marriage pledge to date.

We the undersigned have joined together to present our unified message and plea to the Justices of the United States Supreme Court regarding the matter of marriage.

We are Protestant, Catholic, and Orthodox Christian pastors, clergy, lay leaders and Jewish leaders, who collectively represent millions of people in our specific churches, parishes, denominations, synagogues and media ministry outreaches. Marriage transcends our various theological differences and unites us together in one voice.

We affirm that any judicial opinion which purports to redefine marriage will constitute an unjust law, as Martin Luther King Jr. described such laws in his letter from the Birmingham Jail.

We are Christians who love America and who respect the legitimate rule of law.

However, *we will not honor any decision by the Supreme Court which will force us to violate a clear biblical understanding of marriage as solely the union of one man and one woman.*

We affirm that Marriage, as existing solely between one man and one woman, precedes civil government. Though affirmed, fulfilled, and elevated by faith, the truth that marriage can exist only between one man and one woman is not based solely on religion but on the Natural Law, written on the human heart.

We implore this Court to not step outside of its legitimate authority and unleash religious persecution and discrimination against people of faith. We will be forced to choose between the state and our conscience, which is informed by clear biblical and church doctrine and the natural created order.

On this choice, we must pledge obedience to our Creator. While there are many things we can endure, any attempt to redefine marriage is a line we cannot and will not cross.

This statement is followed by a list of eighty-seven key national religious and church leaders who are from among the thousands who signed the marriage pledge.[2] At the bottom of the full-page article, a scripture verse is printed in bold letters:

> But Peter and the apostles answered, we must obey God rather than man. (Acts 5:29)

On June 26, 2015, the nine Supreme Court justices voted 5-4 to strike down any type of ban on same-sex marriages in all fifty states, thus legalizing same-sex so-called marriages as the law of the land. The front-page headline of the *Houston Chronicle* newspaper on June 27, 2015, read, "Justices: Marriage for All." Other articles throughout the same edition of the newspaper read:

- "Gay Couples Line Up to Wed—Relish Long-Awaited Right"
- "After Historic Ruling, Gays Now Share in Essential Right"
- "A Rainbow of Emotion"
- "Gay Couples Obtaining Marriage Licenses Thought It Would Never Come"
- "Parker[3] Cheers Joyous Day for America"

This ruling is in direct opposition to what the Bible teaches about marriage. God's intention is for marriage to be between one man and one woman for life. He ordained marriage for Bill and Jill, not Larry and Harry or Jan and Ann.

The Supreme Court ruling has generated much dialogue. We all have engaged in conversations and have listened to various commentaries and discussions. In my circle of acquaintances, one comment that surfaces repeatedly goes like this, "I can't believe this

---

2   For more information contact Common Good Foundation (757-620-1615), Liberty Counsel (800-671-1776), Vision America Action (866-522-5582).

3   Houston Mayor Annise Parker is the first openly gay mayor of a major American city. She and her longtime lesbian partner were "married" in California less than a year before this ruling.

has happened in our country!" I can! We must all understand that when God is taken out of anything, it begins to decay—destruction follows close behind and eventually leads to death. Whether it is a marriage, a church, the government, or whatever, it begins to go downhill rapidly.

In Romans 1:28 (NASB), we find, "And just as they did not see fit to acknowledge God any longer, God gave them over to a depraved mind, to do those things which are not proper." And then 2 Timothy 3:18 (KJV) reads, "So do these also resist the truth: men of corrupt minds, reprobate concerning the faith." The words *depraved* and *reprobate* refer to those who knowingly refuse to submit to the truth of God and instead replace Him and His authority with their own unrighteous thinking. Notice carefully God's response—He gives them over to their own reprobate thinking.

When a people (individual or group) continually and deliberately turn their backs on God and His ways, there comes a time when God steps back and says in essence, "Okay, if that's what you want, go your way—and see where it gets you." That's where Galatians 6:7 (NASB) comes in: "Whatever a man sows, this he will also reap."

It is worth the time to read the verses just preceding and following Romans 1:28, which was printed above. Here is Romans 1:24–32 (NASB). Does this sound like an up-to-date description of America today?

> Therefore God gave them over in the lusts of their hearts to impurity, so that their bodies would be dishonored among them. For they exchanged the truth of God for a lie, and worshiped and served the creature rather than the Creator, who is blessed forever. Amen.
>
> For this reason God gave them over to degrading passions; for their women exchanged the natural function for that which is unnatural, and in the same way also the men abandoned the natural function of the woman and burned in their desire toward one another, men with men committing indecent acts and receiving in their own persons the due penalty of their error.

> And just as they did not see fit to acknowledge God any longer, God gave them over to a depraved mind, to do those things which are not proper, being filled with all unrighteousness, wickedness, greed, evil; full of envy, murder, strife, deceit, malice; they are gossips, slanderers, haters of God, insolent, arrogant, boastful, inventors of evil, disobedient to parents, without understanding, untrustworthy, unloving, unmerciful; and although they know the ordinance of God, that those who practice such things are worthy of death, they not only do the same, but also give hearty approval to those who practice them.

What can we as Christians expect when many of our government leaders are depraved people of a reprobate mind? If we open our eyes to reality, we see evidence of depraved minds from more than just Supreme Court justices and/or government leaders. Even prior to the Supreme Court decision, a rapidly growing number of states had passed legislation to legalize same-sex marriage in their state. Our country has sown the seeds of anti-Christianity, antifamily, and antigodliness, and we are now reaping the results. Let's face it—we cannot put all the blame on *them*. Too many of us Christian frogs have sat in the pot of unconcern and complacency too long, and we are being cooked!

What does the Bible teach about marriage? In the Old Testament, we see where God institutes marriage in Genesis 2:24 (NIV):

> For this reason a man will leave his father and mother and be united to his wife, and they will become one flesh.

And in the New Testament in Matthew 19:4–6 (NIV), Jesus says,

> Haven't you read… that in the beginning the Creator made them male and female, and said, "For this reason a man will leave his father and mother and be united to his wife, and the two will become one flesh? So they are no longer two,

but one. Therefore, what God has joined together, let man not separate.

The same-sex-marriage ruling that was just made into law is blatantly opposed to God's Word and the Christian fiber of our nation. It is actually a misnomer to speak of same-sex unions as "marriage"—by biblical definition, it does not qualify.

A huge concern I have is, What's next? If our Supreme Court can declare one law that is exactly contrary to God's Law, what will be next? What kind of legislation could be considered and passed when those making the decisions are depraved and have a reprobate mind? It is already being said that polygamy could be legalized on the same basis of individual rights as same-sex marriage was passed. I shudder to think what might follow! What about pedophilia? Incest? Rape? A reprobate mind has no conscience—it is an ugly thing!

How ridiculous! How anti-Christian! How ludicrous and asinine! How sick! Remember, without God, everything falls apart, decays; and death and destruction are the results.

In a matter of a few days after the Supreme Court ruling, President Obama visited Africa, spending time in Kenya. Although his advisors were not in favor of his doing so, in an address delivered while Obama was present, Kenyan President Kenyatta alluded to the new law, stating Kenya has some "differences" with the United States. What a well-deserved slap in the face for America! In Kenya, homosexual acts are illegal, punishable by up to fourteen years in prison. What a contrast with "Christian" America! Shame, shame on us!

Have you ever seen a football game played on a field with no markings on it? No boundary lines? No end zones? No yard markers? No referees? If two teams played a game on this type of field, what would happen? There would be total chaos, confusion, and injuries. Frustration would be the norm; anarchy and disorder would reign. The lines, referees, and rules all establish order and stability to the game. That is what God's Word (the Bible) and His rules and regulations give us. His laws—given to us out of His love—give purpose, order, and stability to life and serve to protect us. God is a holy God; His standards are righteous. All of God's laws are for our benefit and blessing. They are not just suggestions—they are commands.

Like caring parents love their children and want the best for them, God loves us and wants the best for us too. What are the best things in life? One thing, for sure, all the money in the world can't buy them.

- You can buy a house, but not a home.
- You can buy a lover, but not true love.
- You can buy all the weapons in the world, but not real peace.
- You can buy the best mattress, but not a good night's sleep
- You can buy medicine, but not your health.
- You can buy acquaintances, but not true friendship.
- You can buy church buildings, but not your salvation.
- You can buy books, but not true wisdom.
- You can buy a party, but not true happiness.

And the list goes on and on.

This is a time in history when believers in Christ are going to be tested. Our foundation of faith is going to be tried over and over, and we must stand strong. God's people must lock arms with God and each other in prayer and commitment and remain faithful as we pray for God to bless America and turn our nation back to Him.

The issue of religious liberty is likely going to gear up and be highly controversial. Will our religious freedoms be allowed to stand? Will we be willing to stand true to God's Word regardless of the cost? As our culture moves away from God, we as believers will face more and more criticism, opposition, exclusion, and pressure. Outright persecution may be right around the corner. How will we respond?

I refuse to stay comfortable in the pot and be mesmerized by the never-ending bubbles and the ever-warming waters. Let's together take a giant leap out of the pot and let's get on it!

I have a dim but growing hope in my heart—maybe this Supreme Court decision will be the wake-up call for the believers of America to turn our collective face to our Lord, calling on Him to revive us and save our nation. I pray that the winds of revival will sweep over our nation in a mighty force as we collectively turn back to God!

> Dear Lord,
>
> I come to You on bended knees with a heavy heart to pray for the United States of America. Lord, our only hope is You! I confess my sins of arrogance, complacency, and a lackadaisical attitude toward the sinfulness of our country and ask Your forgiveness. I know the only answer to the spiritual decay and downward spiral of our nation is that we confess our sins, turn from our wicked ways, and petition You to save America! Lord, drain the pots full of self-centered frogs that are numb to what is going on and renew our hearts with a passion that will turn our country back to You. Bring our nation back to the foot of the cross and restore us as a people so that the United States of America will be the catalyst to start a worldwide revival. Thank you, Lord—and please, God, bless America. Amen.

The Public Schools

In 1950, the National Education Association did a national survey of schools asking them to list the top disciplinary issues in their schools. Their research and findings indicated that their main problems were running in the halls, talking in the classrooms, throwing trash on campus, chewing gum, cutting in line, cheating on tests, and making noise in the cafeteria. In 2012, the same survey indicated that the problems were rape, assault on teachers, carrying weapons, bullying, suicide, drugs, teen pregnancy, and gangs.

Assaults on teachers and violence in many forms have increased over 100 percent in the last twenty years. Why is this?

Do a little research for yourself. Go back and look at the statistics regarding the well-being of students in our schools—discipline, crime rate, and academic achievement before and after 1963. That was the year of the US Supreme Court milestone ban on school prayer. As a result of lawsuits filed against the teaching of religion and religious practices in our public schools, prayer was removed from our schools! This was the turning point, the before-and-after marker—God was removed, and it has been a downhill slide ever since!

Are commencement speakers free to mention God or Jesus in their presentations today? What happens when a kid wears a T-shirt to school with a Christian message printed on it? Are our schools safer for our students? Have we lowered the dropout rate? Are our students achieving higher academic standards than ever before? The adverse effects are obvious! It bears repeating: when you remove God, everything goes bad, and the pot is full of miserable frogs. Look at where we are today! Get the picture?

And there's more to come! Now that same-sex marriage is the law of the land, the LGBT agenda will expand as many of us have feared. In fact, it has already begun. Not satisfied with having won their "right" to marry, their next move is to see that everyone else adopts their view and celebrates with them.

Their primary target will be children. A friend recently shared how, in her granddaughter's school in another Texas town, the elementary school principal instructed the faculty to begin indoctrinating their students of every grade level to accept same-sex marriages as normative. The teachers were told to say to their students, "Don't tell your parents, they won't understand." So how did my friend know about this incident? Her daughter is a teacher in that school.

Much of Canada approved gay marriage almost a decade ago. In an online blog, a Canadian gay activist wrote,

> I have come to indoctrinate your children into my LGBTQ agenda (and I'm not a bit sorry). I want to make your children like people like me and my family, even if that goes against the way you have interpreted the teachings of your religion. I would be happy—delighted, overjoyed I tell you—to cause those children to disagree with their families on the subject of LGBTQ people.

An American gay activist voiced similar sentiments in an online story in 2011: "We want educators to teach future generations to accept queer sexuality. In fact, our very future depends upon it. Recruiting children? You bet we are."

Speaking at an LGBT educational conference in April, a teacher of primary grades told other educators about her success in changing the perspectives of her kindergarten students by engaging them in "difficult conversations" and reading books to them about same-sex couples. A photograph of her and her lesbian partner is displayed on her desk, and she frequently and intentionally shares experiences involving her family with the young students. She proudly reports they soon accept her lifestyle as normal. Dr. James Dobson feels this scenario is much more common than we would realize, but most teachers are too cautious to admit it openly. Chilling, isn't it!

If all this were not bad enough, there's even more. We haven't even touched the tip of the iceberg. There is a growing trend popping up in news headlines across the country—parents choosing to raise their child genderless, or as the opposite gender, according to the child's preference. For example, if a little girl prefers to enter into the realm of activities usually associated with little boys, we used to just think of her as a tomboy. Today's parents might allow and even encourage her to take on the male role in clothing, hairstyle, name change (referring to her as a boy, their son). How sad! Transgender children—all with parental blessing! How far will the reprobate mind go?

One prominent example is a fourteen-year-old biological boy who, with his heterosexual parents' assistance, has passed himself off as a girl since age two. His name was changed to Jazz. He has "become a girl," wearing girl clothes and hairdo. Jazz has written a children's book about his transgender experience and now, along with his mother, has a reality TV show. I wonder—which restroom does he use at school? Does he go to boys PE class or girls PE class? I highly suspect the school allows his choice to reign.

How confusing will this be to our children and grandchildren? How complicated will their friendships become? How will dating relationships be affected? Who will be invited to sleepovers? Will it become the norm to just choose your gender after birth? Will biological gender be completely ignored? What craziness—no, what depravity!

Our world has turned upside down! Marriage has fallen out of favor with many heterosexual couples, who prefer instead to live together without being married. In contrast, homosexual couples, no longer satisfied to just live together, want to be married. Pick your gender—change your mind whenever you feel like it. Where will it all lead? Further and further away from God!

Back in 1963, when all this got a foothold with the Supreme Court ban on school prayer, there was a segment of the Christian community that did not remain silent. There was an outcry against the ruling by some churches, pastors, and other religious leaders across the country. Some rallied their churches and denominations to fight the ban. However, it wasn't enough. The majority of Christians thought, *This is the good old USA. They won't really take prayer out of our public schools. That will never happen!* At the time, every church in America should have pulled out all the stops and mounted an all-out, no-holds-barred effort to fight the prayer ban!

What happened? They were relaxing in a pot of warm water with other Christian frogs, fascinated with the bubbles around them, enjoying the gradually increasing rise in temperature, watching a football game on black-and-white TV. They played the role of the frog in the pot to perfection!

Government

We are all familiar with the phrase, "In God We Trust." It is printed on our paper currency; and every time I read it, I pray, "Please, Lord, let it be so!" Our early history reflects the fact that our founding fathers and government system were totally dependent upon our Lord. Many congressional meetings were just prayer groups that also included government business. A primary emphasis in forming our government was faith in God and trust in Jesus Christ. Our nation was established on the knees of dedicated men, praying for God's leadership, and built on the hope that all Americans trust in God! Do you hear this type of commitment to God and dependence upon His divine leadership coming out of Washington, DC, today?

How is your confidence level when it comes to Washington, DC? What about your trust in our government? There was a time that it was an honored and respected institution, but there has been a debacle never before experienced in all of its glorious history. *Dishonesty, bribes, greed, corruption, undercover deals, chaos, mistrust, fraud,* and just plain *lies* seem to be words associated with our American politics. Oops, I shouldn't say *lies.* Today's political figures don't lie—they misspeak and misremember!

Where are the honor and pride that once were the standard when you mentioned the presidency and the American government? When I was a boy about twelve years old, it was announced that President Dwight D. Eisenhower was going to be in Houston, Texas. I was so excited that the president of the United States was actually going to be in our city. I got on a city bus and rode it downtown by myself so I could get a place to stand to see our president as his motorcade passed by.

I did see him. It was a very impressive and exciting sight for this twelve-year-old. The president's flag-covered limo was escorted by policemen on motorcycles. Tons of people lined the street along with me. As he passed in front of me, I waved, and he was also waving. I was sure he waved just at me. I was so proud to have seen with my own eyes a real live president of the United States of America. I liked Ike then, and I still like Ike, just because of that memory!

President Harry Truman officially established a National Day of Prayer in 1952, and in 1988, President Ronald Reagan established a permanent date for the NDP—it is now the first Thursday in May. Praise God, our country at least still has a National Day of Prayer!

The four basic foundational pillars of our society—the church, home/marriage/family, public schools, and government have played a major role in holding our country together and steady through the merciful hand of God. But all four today are eroding, cracking, and shaking. People have lost trust and feel insecure. As a result, they look for other things to anesthetize their pain, distract their minds, and help them escape their fear. It is my personal opinion that the discontent and fear in our society have led to the unbelievable growth of sports and entertainment. Miserable frogs wanting to get away from it all may consider sports and entertainment venues a good place to hop to. Then they can just sit in their own customized pots and soak it all in!

Our hallowed American institutions are trembling and on the verge of collapse. We've tried politics, government reform programs, and billions of dollars thrown at our problems, but things seem to change very little. In general, our country has sat in a gradually heating pot of water and has been hypnotized by the ungodly things of this world, and we are now suffering the paralyzing consequences. We have examined each one of the foundational pillars and found that God has been removed and assigned a place of nonimportance. There are so many pots around filled with miserable frogs. In God we trust—really?

One of Satan's greatest tricks is to get believers sidetracked so they won't focus on the main thing. A good illustration of this is found in Meredith Wilson's 1962 musical *The Music Man*. This is the story about a smooth-talking self-proclaimed con man, Professor Harold Hill. His main goal in life is to swindle the good citizens of River City, Iowa, out of every nickel they own. He plans to do this by selling them brass band instruments (which he does not have) and fancy uniforms (which he does not have) and music lessons (which he does not have—nor can he play a note on any instrument) and to form a marching band (which he knows nothing about).

Armed with a gift of gab and false credentials, he ignites mass concern among the parents of River City because there is a new pool hall being built in their fair city. In the song "You Got Trouble," he describes what could happen should the citizens choose a pool hall over a boys' marching band. As he is describing the cussing, smoking, drinking, and general debauchery of a pool hall, he sings this line that refers to a pool table: "Pool, that starts with p, that rhymes with t, that stands for trouble." The illustrative point here is that the River City citizens focus on the evils of a pool hall and are too preoccupied to check the authenticity and honesty of Professor Howard Hill.

Professor Harold Hill convinces the citizenry to go with the boys' marching band. While he is selling band instruments and uniforms hand over fist and collecting tons of money, at the same time, he is plotting his midnight exit from River City. Everything is going just fine until he meets Marion the librarian, falls in love, and—get the DVD, you will enjoy it. *The Music Man* is fun, ends great, and everybody is happy. It is a fun fictional story.

Churches can be caught in the same hot pot—but then it's not fun, and it's not fiction! Focusing on the wrong things will make a church vulnerable to losing everything to a slick-talking, silver-tongued, crooked charlatan named Professor Satan.

Life in a church does not have to be like that. It is way better when the star of the show is Jesus Christ and the church is turned on to Him. He guides and directs His church. He also maintains the water in the pot at the perfect temperature. The frogs of the church are not lulled into inactivity but are on the front lines of combat, guarding and advancing the kingdom of God.

When Adolf Hitler was planning his conquest of Europe, he knew his biggest threat and foe would be the true church of Jesus Christ. Hitler knew Christianity well and how it could influence individuals to the point that they would not follow the Nazi government. He was keenly aware that Christians would oppose his "superior-race" mandate because it was directly opposed to Christian teachings. He made an elaborate plan to destroy any trace of Christianity as he established what he called the German Reformation Movement.

This movement was dedicated to getting rid of the Old Testament, "with its Jewish morality," and purging the New Testament of all "superstitious" passages. From September 21, 1933, to May 31, 1934, there was a highly organized and powerful German blitzkrieg against every aspect of the Christian church. A dedicated band of brave pastors rose up in protest, led by giants of the faith like Dietrich Bonhoeffer, Karl Barth, and other strong and committed men of God.

On May 29–31, 1934, a group of pastors, theologians, and other Christian leaders met in Germany, city of Wuppertal, Barmen, to pray and write "The Theological Declaration of Barmen." The document was written to help believers withstand the challenges of the Nazi party and of the so-called German Christians. The latter was a popular movement that falsely taught there was no conflict between Christianity and the ideals of Hitler's National Socialism.

The rise of Hitler and the Nazi party in Germany threatened not just the civil and political rights of Germans but also matters of Christian conscience and faith. The Nazi government installed its own handpicked delegate, Dr. August Jäger, a volatile anti-Christian, as the supreme leader of the German Church. He declared that it was illegal to preach sermons opposing any part of the Nazi movement and issued an edict called the Muzzling Order.

In protest, the pastors, theologians, university professors, and other believers secretly gathered in Barmen, Germany, to compose a document they felt had to explain the theological errors inherent in Nazi state control of Christianity. They did meet and, in a daring way, produced "The Declaration of Barmen," which was a bold statement against the Nazi movement, the German Reformation Movement, German Christians, and the Muzzling Order. Signing it and being a part of the conference meetings were equivalent to signing one's own death warrants individually and one's family's.

If you have a chance, it is inspiring and educational to read this six-point declaration. Each of the six statements begins with scripture, followed by an explanation of the text, and then concluding with a statement that begins with, "We reject the false doctrine of..." This is followed by a bold explanation of their godly stance against the Nazi claims. Some very disturbing facts about this entire scenario are the following:

1. All the churches in Germany knew about the Nazi movement and the so-called German Christian campaign. They did very little against the German Christians; some even adopted the Nazi view and espoused and preached it from their Christian pulpits.

2. Germany was coming out of a very difficult economic time, and Hitler was bringing more prosperity and well-being to the country than they had experienced in years. People trusted Hitler and enjoyed the new wealth and prosperity their nation was experiencing. New jobs were being created, stores had items on their shelves, and things looked good. (The unethical and diabolical methods Hitler used to accomplish this prosperity were not known by the German people. The methods and cost of lives did not matter to the Nazis.)

The terrible truth is that the Christians in Germany were duped and misguided and did not realize what was going on until it was far too late. The water in their pot was too hot and sapped their strength, diminished their thinking, and completely paralyzed them.

I am not blaming the genuine German believers. I have thought long and hard about how I would react if I had been one of them. My research has helped me realize how difficult a situation they were in. The ruthless and demonic government of the Nazis inflicted punishment on anyone who resisted them at all or were considered a danger to the state. The age or gender of the violator had no bearing on the extent of the punishment applied. People faced all types of hardships, which included arrest, imprisonment of entire families in different prison camps, torture, and in some cases, execution. The Nazis were definitely in control of everything and ruled with a studded iron fist and the German iron cross.

What happened in Germany in the years that followed? It is a terrible and horrific history that is almost impossible to understand and believe. Could it happen in the churches in America? Have there been "theological adjustments" by denominational groups? Has the gospel been more boldly preached or set aside for something more current? Have we become more knowledgeable and discerning about the truth of God's Word, or would we readily accept distortions and falsehoods without even being aware of the deception? Has the water in the pot of our churches become so hot and numbing that error and indifference have crept in?

Here are a few biblical truths this situation should teach all of us:

1. When God is removed from any country, organization, family, or pot of frogs, decline and decay always occur and eventually lead to death.
2. Whatever a man (country, church, nation) sows, they will also reap.
3. The true German believers were oblivious to what was going on, and many were enjoying the water in the pot of prosperity and change.
4. We must always be aware of the possibilities of being in Satan's pot too long.

When we are in Satan's pot too long, these things happen:

- Gradually, the warming water feels good.
- The longer we stay in the water, the weaker we become.
- The bubbles distract us.
- We get so comfortable we think that *it* will never happen.

The true church of Jesus Christ will always survive. The answer to any question and solution to any problem is always available through Jesus. The only way to avoid being the frog in the pot is to make sure you are always snuggled up to Jesus in His ever-caring and protecting arms. Jesus continues to rescue frogs and drain pots.

Besides the deceivingly warm and bubbling waters of a pot, a church can begin to change their presentations of the gospel and their methods so more people will come to the church. This practice could aptly be called *playing to the crowd*. In other words, doing what it takes to get folks there even if you have to compromise your spiritual stance. This creates an absolute no-win situation.

People desire the approval of other people—that's just human nature. However, to become controlled by a desire for approval is to play the part of the old man in the following fable.

> There was an elderly man traveling with a boy and a donkey. As they walked through a village, the man was leading the donkey and the boy was walking behind. The townspeople said the man was an old fool for not riding, so to please them he climbed up on the animal's back.
>
> When they came to the next village, the people said the old man was cruel to let the child walk while he enjoyed the ride. So to please them he got off and set the boy on the donkey's back and continued on his way.
>
> In the third village, people accused the child of being lazy for making the old man walk, and the suggestion was made that they both ride. So to please the villagers, the man climbed on along with the boy, and they set off again, both riding the donkey.

In the fourth village, the townspeople were indignant at the cruelty to the donkey because he was made to carry two people. The frustrated man was last seen walking with the boy, both of them helping carry the donkey as they went down the road!

What a graphic way to describe the danger of playing to the crowd. We all have too many different pairs of eyes looking in on our life to keep everyone's approval intact. At the end of the day, the pair of eyes that monumentally matter the most are the ones looking down from heaven. It is only the deep satisfaction of going for broke in a God-enabled, God-directed assault upon life that can keep individuals and churches from seeking and needing others' approval. Churches can become so enthralled with the approval of others that they sacrifice their spiritual integrity in order to keep their approval intact.

When any church is dominated by their desire for the approval of man rather than the approval of Christ, they are in the donkey-carrying business. Obviously, donkeys and frogs don't mix too well!

Let's take a look at these thought-provoking, rhetorical questions about the boiling pots full of frogs that may be found in many churches:

- What are some negative influences that have crept into our churches that are producing adverse affects as the church frogs are comfortably lounging in their pots?
- Could there be biblically erroneous teachings or practices that have been in place so long and practiced for so long that the frogs are numb to the fact that they even exist?
- Are some churches so strangled by debt that they have compromised on teaching biblical truths, thinking to attract more givers?
- Is it possible for the older, more mature frogs to be so comfortable in the warm water of their traditions that they

would rather push out most of the young frogs and eliminate all the tadpoles rather than change?

Rib-bit, rib-bit, rib-bit!

What Then Are We to Do?

Playing the frog in the pot has us in hot water for sure! We've assessed the state of the church, the home/family/marriage, the public schools, and the government and found each to be in shambles! We acknowledge our role in the decline around us. In our neglect and complacency, we recognize ourselves as the proverbial frog in the pot.

Now that we have come to our senses at the very last moment, just before the water temperature reached the boiling point, and have made a frantic leap out of the pot—what do we do?

The book of 1 Peter is a letter the apostle Peter wrote to believers who were beginning to face opposition, which would grow into intense persecution. His words were written to encourage and instruct in preparation for what was to come. The entire book is quite applicable for us today. Only five chapters in length, it is worthy of reading through often. Here are some thoughts based on 1 Peter:

1. Pray for those in rebellion against God.
   Prayer is our most powerful weapon!
2. Love the sinner.
   Let Christ's love within us be evident to all!
3. Be understanding of weaker brothers.
   Fellow believers need our support, not our criticism!
4. Do not bend on the issues.
   God's laws never change—we must not either!
5. Be prepared to suffer for religious liberty.
   Decide your position in advance then stand firm!

6. Stay true to God's Word.
   Live an exemplary life of obedience!
7. With gratitude, accept the opportunity to suffer for Jesus.
   Never forget—He suffered and died for us!

13

From the Heart of Buddy

What a ride!

Have you ever ridden a roller coaster? Perhaps you have to think back awhile. As a teenager, I well remember the mixed feelings of fear, excitement, and anxiety we all experienced as we stood in line waiting our turn on the Wild Thing! We could see the idiots in the front seats holding their arms up in the air as it clickety-clacked its way to the top of the first daring, death-defying descent. Then we heard the screams of the riders, the swoosh of the coaster and watched in amazed dread as the coaster sped up, down, and all around and wondered if we would really ride it.

Finally it was our turn. We handed our ticket to the ticket-taker, sat down in our seats, and lowered the lap bar until it snapped in place. The cars jerked, and we slowly started the ascent as our lives flashed before our eyes. We reached the apex; it slowed. The clickety-clack sounds began to fade, and then—I can't even remember what happened next. (Since you are reading this, I assume you survived too!) It happened so fast! It was over so quickly! I had spent more time standing in line to get on the roller coaster than I did enduring it (that was my sister's second ride—her first and last!). I couldn't wait to get back in line and ride it over and over and over again!

When I was a boy in Houston, Texas, there was an amusement facility named Playland Park. I loved it! To go there was a rare treat for me! Playland Park had a special deal on tickets on the weekends. All ride tickets were normally $.25 each. However, if you bought your tickets before 6:00 p.m., they were $.10 each. I was there on a Friday night before 6:00 p.m., and I bought $3.00 worth of tickets with money I earned shining shoes. I had thirty tickets, and I planned to use all of them riding the Wild Thing, which was the name of their hair-raising, gut-wrenching roller coaster.

However, after about my tenth fling with the Wild Thing, for some reason, it was not as much fun as the first few rides; and it became the *tame thing*. By the time my fifteenth ride was beginning, I was wondering, *Who signed me up for this?* On my next ride, as I descended, I took my remaining tickets and threw them up in the air, all the time wishing I could trade them in for a hot dog and Dr. Pepper! The Wild Thing was definitely over for me. The more I rode the coaster, the fewer thrills it produced. That first spine-tingling, breathtaking, supercharged excitement was definitely gone, and the ride had just become a disappointing letdown.

My sixteen-month ride of visiting 115 churches as a secret church shopper produced just the opposite effect—it never became boring or routine. The more churches I visited, the more fun it was, and the better I got at it. My discernment skills improved, I gained valuable experience and insights, and I enjoyed it more and more. The law of diminishing returns was not relevant at all. The more churches I visited, the more focused I became, and the more our Lord revealed to me. The entire sixteen-month ride was thrilling, and I didn't even have to stand in long lines to get tickets!

The results of seeing God at work during this time were personally rewarding and produced some wonderful outcomes in my own life. But before the "wonderful outcomes," there was a process that was not so pleasant. When the light of God's holiness begins to shine upon us, it exposes negative and ungodly things not previously evident. The closer I walked with God, the more things I discovered in my own life that had to be adjusted. Certain attitudes that were just plain rotten deep within me began to surface. Some of them were stinking up my life and affecting me in ways I didn't previously realize. I didn't like it—not a bit!

Let me back up here to tell my story. It's not a story I'm proud of, but it is a story that needs to be told. It comes from my heart—that's where this chapter got its title.

Earlier in this book, I described how part of my regular church-visiting routine was to pray before each visit. I anticipated experiencing worship services that would be done differently in a variety of settings among many denominations. I sincerely desired to have an open mind as I took it all in. My request to God was that He remove from my heart any preconceived ideas and biases that might cloud my evaluations. I was not naive enough to think I was completely innocent.

It's funny how God answers prayer! What I had in mind was that He would just instantly zap away whatever wrong attitudes I might have. Then—poof!—they would disappear, and I would have a pure heart! That's not what God had in mind at all! His ways are not our ways. I've already alluded to the "wonderful outcome" of this, but we're not there yet. Allow me to continue the story.

Week by week, the more I prayed, sought our Lord's leadership, and visited churches, the more frequent and intense this stench became.

Let me explain further. Early on in my church-visiting project, there were times I would drive into a church parking lot and have a most disturbing thought pop into my head. Verbalized, my thoughts might go something like this:

- This is such a small church—they're probably living in the Dark Ages!
- This is going to be a waste of time—I'm sure I know more about church work than they do!
- I know I won't hear the Bible preached in this denomination!
- This is going to be dullsville for sure!
- This will likely be a pretty snobby bunch!

There were other thoughts—this is just a sample. Then I would immediately think, *Where did a thought like that come from?* Ouch, and shame on me! Where are You, God? I thought You were going to take this away!

The more time I spent in prayer and visiting churches, the more I began to realize I was harboring prejudices and biased thoughts. I have to admit, it caught me by surprise. Was I so conditioned to such thoughts that I was not aware of them? Was it my pride that got in the way? Was I blind to judgmental thinking? My first answer was, *No, not me, of course not! I don't drink, chew, or go with girls that do—I am really a good old boy!*

Our Lord began to reveal to me that was not totally true. Even though I thought I loved everybody and had no prejudices or discriminatory opinions in my heart, the fact was, I did. As the stench grew stronger and more obvious, I began to realize that the really wonderful Christian man I imagined myself to be was not so wonderful after all. I found inside my mind and heart some bad attitudes and preconceived ideas that were decaying in a pit of my pride. In fact, they were stinking up the joint, and the joint was me! The light of His holiness lovingly revealed my faults over a period of several weeks. At this point, I must say how grateful and thankful I am for that!

About six weeks or so into my church-visiting project, I pulled into the parking lot of a church, completely oblivious of what God had in store for me. Unable to locate the church I had originally planned to visit that Sunday morning, I noticed this one and, on the spur of the moment, decided to stop in.

As I walked in the door, I was completely unaware that I was stepping into God's divine appointment. I met the pastor in the foyer. I was soon to learn that he is a wonderful, dedicated man of God who loves his church family and is greatly loved by them in return.

The pastor's sermon was titled "Anyone Can Drink" and centered around the story of the Samaritan woman at the water well in John

4. Jesus, a Jew, engaged her in conversation despite the fact that the Samaritans were hated by the Jews and vice versa. Jesus went out of His way to offer her Living Water.

The pastor made the point that Jesus purposely traveled through Samaria to demonstrate that He had no bias or prejudice, which is the example Christians should adopt and live by. He posed this question to the congregation, "Can you think of any group or race of people you just don't want to meet, or talk to, or sit by, or be associated with, or even pray with?" He continued, "Is there anyone you purposely avoid, talk negatively about, or would not worship with?" He then concluded, "If your answer is *yes* to any of these questions, you harbor prejudice." That nailed me! I was guilty! He then listed the following categories of people to consider our feelings toward them:

- Illegal immigrants
- Wealthy people
- Poor people
- People of color
- Ethnic groups
- Folks with accents
- Sexual orientation
- Body piercers
- Educated
- Uneducated
- Those with big cars
- Those with junker cars
- Bikers
- Tall, short, big, tiny
- Good-looking
- Those not so hot-looking
- Other denominations
- Those in gated communities
- Those in the hood
- Those with tattoos
- Those who wear baggy pants
- Ex-cons
- Long, short, and no hair
- Single, divorced, married
- Interracial marriages
- The old, young, teens

The pastor related this story. He had recently participated as a volunteer decision counselor in a large citywide evangelistic crusade held at a football stadium. When the come-forward invitation was given, scores of people responded. As he stood in his assigned place in front, facing the crowd, he noticed a man walking directly toward him. He was a white man in his late twenties, with long hair and a long beard, tattooed from head to toe, wearing a T-shirt, shorts, and flip-flops.

The pastor confessed that he suddenly wanted to avoid dealing with the tattooed man. His inclination was to look away and step back a bit, hoping the one seeking salvation would approach a different counselor. Shocked that he would feel this way because of the man's appearance, he thought, *This man is a human being, coming to learn about Christ who died on the cross for his sins, and I am so full of prejudice that I don't want to talk to him! God forgive me!*

The stench I discovered in my life emanated from similar prejudices and biases toward certain people and groups. With my prideful air of superiority, I was unable to recognize what was in my heart. Only the light of God's countenance shining in the deepest parts of my soul exposed the decay of discrimination and putrid attitudes I harbored. As the toxic effect threatened to contaminate other parts of my being, I realized there is no Febreze adequate enough to spray on and dissolve the stench. I knew I must have Jesus, the Great Physician, perform a radical, prejudice-ectomy and totally remove the root cause from the depths of my repentant soul.

I called 1-800-FOR-GIVE and scheduled the surgery. The operation was quick, and recovery time was short. His love and care for me is the greatest rehab, and the scar tissue that formed has added strength to my whole being. Now there is a sweet spirit and fragrance in my life that only Jesus can give.

What we think about other people, our attitudes and feelings, plays a part in the choices we make. In other words, our existing prejudices and biases have a huge influence over our actions.

Perhaps all of us are guilty to some degree. I can read over the list the pastor gave and see myself with less-than-ideal attitudes in almost every case. All our thoughts toward others must be placed under the microscope of God's Word to be examined and adjusted according to His standards. As always, the answer to any situation is Jesus Christ. When we do our part to open ourselves up to Him,

He takes over to remove long-suppressed prejudices. Then the sweet aroma of God's love and presence is evident.

I am so thankful that God answered my prayer to remove unrighteous notions and biases from my heart! His timing was perfect—then from the early stages of my church research, I was able to move on from an unbiased perspective. Despite the rather painful process, the *wonderful outcome* was well worth it all!

By the way, at the beginning of my story about attending a church that was not on my schedule, I purposely did not mention that the pastor is an African American with what appeared to be a 99.9 percent African American congregation. In my eyes, he is a giant of the faith! I will never forget what God did in my life on that day! I called him the following week to share my story and express my appreciation. We had a great conversation and praised God together!

I have seen discrimination of various types demonstrated to some degree in churches I visited. Not only have I seen it, but I have experienced it too. I was in a very formal and traditional large church where all men were wearing suits and ties and the women were definitely dressed for "high church." As was my custom throughout all my church visits, I was wearing jeans—nice jeans— and a shirt with the tail out. After being ignored in the foyer for twenty minutes, I finally entered the worship center to take my seat about five minutes before the service began.

As I headed down the aisle toward the front, as also was my custom, an usher stopped me. He motioned with his arm as he told me there were "seats in the back." At least it was the first time I had been spoken to since I arrived. I thanked him with a smile but continued down the aisle and sat on the fourth row—just stubborn, I guess! Although I can't know for sure, I had the distinct impression that the "inappropriateness" of my attire prompted the usher's direction! I couldn't help but think of James 2:2–4, 9 (NASB):

> For if a man comes into your assembly with a gold ring and dressed in fine clothes, and there also comes in a poor man

in dirty clothes, and you pay special attention to the one who is wearing the fine clothes, and say, 'You sit here in a good place,' and you say to the poor man, 'You stand over there, or sit down by my footstool,' have you not made distinctions among yourselves, and become judges with evil motives?

But if you show partiality, you are committing sin and are convicted by the law as transgressors.

Maybe that lesson should be included in the church-ushers handbook!

I have a dear friend named Richard Headrick, whom I consider a wild man for Jesus! He and his wife, Gina, are dedicated servants of our Lord. I don't have enough paper in this book to adequately describe Richard—public speaker, businessman, CEO, filmmaker, author, founder of the Hope Foundation, founder of the Good Samaritan Foundation, founder and president of the Christian motorcycle organization called Hellfighters International, Mission at the Cross, and much more—get the picture? An incredible guy!

Richard wrote a very revealing book titled *America's Churches Through the Eyes of a Bum: The Story Nobody Wanted Told.* Since 1989, he and Gina have spent many of their weekends hanging out on the lawns and parking lots of America's largest churches, dressed not as fine upstanding citizens but rather in old tattered and dirty clothes more typical of the homeless. It is in this guise that they have experienced the shocking response of today's Sunday-morning-churchgoing crowds to people who "don't look like they do." These different people were rejected, despised, and looked down upon by many but loved and cared for by some. The book is their story of how God's Golden Rule is no longer being applied to the down-and-out folks who wind up on the doorsteps of churches attended by the up-and-in folks.

The first chapter, called "The First Church of the Frozen Chosen," describes their routine. Richard and Gina meet with the pastor in advance then, with his support and approval, dress like bums and hang around the church property during the weekend.

Then at the Sunday morning worship service, the pastor announces a guest speaker. Richard and Gina, still wearing their bum attire, walk down the aisle to the podium, and deliver a message from Matthew 7: "Do unto others as you would have them do unto you."

The 330 pages of the book tell story after story of how the Headrick bums were treated by the "church folks" at the First Self-Righteous Churches. Quite a convicting read. It reeks with prejudice, bias, isolation, discrimination, and other negative attitudes and actions demonstrated by Christian people. "Do unto others" is not just a suggestion—it is a command! I wonder how I would react if they showed up at my church. Would I call security to escort them off the property? Would I welcome them with open arms? Would I seat them at the back of the worship center? Would I direct them to our Helping Hands benevolence office?

Many actions a church takes are governed by prejudices and traditions. I think the older a congregation gets and the longer they have been "doing it our way," the more likely it is for prejudices to develop and be sustained. We must depend upon the Lord to reveal these errors and then correct them for His glory and the advancement of His kingdom.

I have observed in more than a few instances that there are churches against change in any form, regardless of positive results of the change. They just want it their way, no matter what. Let me illustrate.

I was on a team to help an older church rebound and get back to being a dynamic, Christ-honoring church in their community. The church had been in existence for over 40 years, and in their glory days, their Sunday attendance was between 300 and 350 people. Through the years, the attendance had dropped to about 50. They called our church for help. After a period of prayer, a few meetings, and an evaluation process, our church assessment team (CAT)/ mission team responded with an excited *yes!*

We met many times with their church leadership to pray and plan together. We decided the first step was to take a survey of the community. Over a period of six weeks of research, denominational office input, door-to-door visits, weekly meetings, demographic studies, and more prayer, we were finally at a point where we could initiate a plan of action.

We enlisted a volunteer construction team, God's Builders, as well as other church volunteers, to improve the physical facilities. This included conducting general cleaning, painting classrooms, repairing roofs, replacing outdated lighting, installing new carpet, and painting the exteriors.

Our surveys revealed there were many kids in the neighborhood and that 87 percent of the residents, within five miles of the church, were Hispanic. We decided to put on a Saturday funfest for the community, focusing on attracting kids. We knew if we could get the kids there, the parents would come with them. We were particularly focused on young families. To make the funfest more appealing, we decided that everything would be free. Thinking this would be a great way to reintroduce the church to the community, we went door to door passing out colorful flyers, posted signs throughout the community, and publicized in every way we could.

The funfest was going to be held outdoors on the church property—with rides, games, bouncy things, contests, clowns, live music, hot dogs, drinks, cotton candy, popcorn, and a really nice gift bag for all adults with a Christian CD, a tract with the plan of salvation, mints, gum, and information about the church.

The big day arrived—our Lord provided perfect weather—and the funfest was an overwhelming success with over four hundred people attending! We had to make two additional trips to the grocery store to get extra hot-dog buns and drinks, and it all worked out beautifully. The next day, awards for some of the contests were handed out during the worship service, which helped produce a huge crowd—the largest in fifteen years. Since 87 percent of the community was Hispanic, about the same percentage was in the worship service.

The church began to grow, and there was an obvious need for Hispanic staff leadership. Our mission team and CAT continued to meet with the church leadership and their deacons but soon began to sense that something was wrong. It appeared that our teams were more excited about what was happening than the leadership of the church.

To make a long story short, they resented the fact that we created a situation where the Hispanics were "taking over their church." You have probably guessed by now—the original church was an aging all-white congregation. Racial prejudice had reared its ugly head! The church people did not rejoice that whole families were being brought under the teaching of God's Word and that the numbers were steadily growing. They only wanted to bring back the old days when it was "just us and none of them." That was the end of our ministry there—we let them know we could not assist them any longer according to their goals. This was a lose-lose-lose situation. The local church, the community, and the family of God all lost. Eleven months later, the church dissolved. How sad! How tragically sad!

We've all known of similar situations. Frequently the scenario is "the neighborhood changed"—meaning, another racial group moved into an all-white neighborhood. The white population dwindles. The church has no interest in reaching out to the "others," and the church struggles to stay afloat. Some see the solution as relocating to a new all-white area or merging with a megachurch. But often they hang on, selfishly refusing to embrace the community and clinging to their how-we've-always-been way of thinking. Funeral by funeral, the church dies a slow death. What a sad and disgraceful commentary!

Racial prejudice is still around. At times we think we are making progress toward it being eradicated, but time after time, incidents in the news remind us that is not the case. Let's face it—we live in a fallen world. Racial prejudice is sin. We will never entirely eliminate racial prejudice from the world! Sin abounds in the world!

But what about in the family of God? We are "*in* the world but not *of* the world," according to the prayer of Jesus in John 17. We march to the beat of a different Drummer—we are set apart from the world. There is no place in the church for racial prejudice and segregation of races!

I am happy to say that observing racial diversity in many of today's churches was one of the highlights of my church visiting! It is an area where our young people seem to be leading the way. Among the newer churches—the ones that are mostly made up of young families and young singles—I found many races and nationalities represented. What a wonderful experience it was to worship together with people of all colors and ethnic backgrounds!

However, among older churches, all-white congregations were the norm. Some might have a sprinkling of minority races, but this would be the exception. Perhaps there are several reasons for this: (1) Older generations grew up in a day of segregation and white dominance, making it difficult to break the chains of the past. (2) A church established as a white church with all-white leadership is not likely to attract nonwhites. (3) People become more resistant to change the older they get. None of these are valid excuses in God's eyes, but they are likely reasons for the situations as they are.

> Therefore go and make disciples of [*all*] nations, baptizing them in the name of the Father and the Son and the Holy Spirit. (Matthew 28:19)

The word *all* means "everyone"!

Here's a story of a pastor and church who have taken very seriously the words of Matthew 28:19 to evangelize all nations, thus bringing them into the church. Like many areas of America, Houston has become a very diverse city or, as some would say, a melting pot. More and more neighborhoods are a mixture of races, nationalities, and ethnic groups.

The story begins with a landlocked church relocating to make way for expansion and growth. After construction of a building and opening their doors to the world, the relocated members were surprised at who came through the doors. It seems that, previously unknown to them, they were surrounded by people of many races and nationalities. The members were not exactly happy with their "new look," and one by one, they began to bail. Within two or three years, the church folded—another tragedy for the body of Christ!

There is a silver lining—that's just the first chapter of the story! God had someone waiting in the wings who was not only willing but eager to take up the ball and run with it, a man who had served on the staff of the failed church. With a heart for reaching *all* people and a wife who shared his fervor, a plan was set into motion. Together they sought the Lord about planting a new church in a nearby area and prayed that He would send the people from "every tribe and tongue and people and nation." God answered their prayer!

Today, ten years later, they are a thriving church of five or six hundred people of the most cross-cultural blend I think I have ever seen in one congregation. They are heavily involved in missions outside of their walls, and their youth group is amazing!

When the men came forward to receive the offering plates on the Sunday I visited, the pastor asked one of the gentlemen to lead the offertory prayer, first in English and then in his heart language. Although all their services are in English, they often invite the worshipers to use their mother tongue if they want. When questioned about the methods used to bring in such a diverse group, the pastor testifies that all he did was pray, and God sent them in—just like the animals came to Noah into the ark! What a lovely picture of the body of Christ!

In visiting another church, the first thing I noticed as I entered was the ethnic diversity of the people arriving on the scene, some dressed in their native attire. I have been in this church many times and know the pastor well. The church is among the largest in the region and is at least forty years old. Although I know this to be a congregation that has never been opposed to other races of people, I had never seen so many present before. After the service, in a private conversation with the pastor, I remarked to him how impressed I was with the ethnic diversity of his congregation. He told me, "If you are going to reach a community for Christ, your church has to look like the community." Right on! I heartily agree!

It was not the time to discuss further, but I got the impression that the church had intentionally reached out to bring in this diverse group—it didn't just happen. What did they do? How did they go about it? Intrigued with the possibilities, I contacted the church later on to get some answers.

This church is located in a rapidly developing suburb of Houston, where most of the rather affluent residents are young to middle-aged professionals with growing families, well educated and successful. The same could be said for the church people.

Here's what I learned from one of the pastoral staff members.

When the present pastor came on board, he began to notice that the ethnic mix of the church didn't match the ethnic mix of the community. This was a concern to him because it was his desire and goal to reach the community for Christ. In 2003, a survey of the church indicated they were 82 percent white. Other research showed their suburban city to be 48 percent white. Although the church was not a totally white church, they fell far short of matching the community figure.

The pastoral leadership and congregation didn't know what to do to bring about the change, so they prayed and asked God to show them what to do! Yes! They prayed! I was thrilled to hear this answer! They didn't strategize and come up with a list of ten steps for reaching minorities—they went right to the Source for the answer! Then they waited! Another great move—they actually expected God to answer, and they waited until He did!

As they continued to pray and wait, the ones they were hoping for began to come—half of all new people coming into the church were nonwhite people! The church began to encourage minorities with what they term "elevate the qualified." In other words, they purposely placed qualified nonwhite people in positions of leadership, especially in very visible roles. This would include singing in the choir, welcoming guests, handing out bulletins, ushering, making announcements, or any other volunteer role for which they have been adequately trained. They seek to have a good representation as deacons and feature them in videos of church activities. The message they want to get across to nonwhite visitors is, *I could serve here—this could be "my" church.*

Is it working out? They are definitely moving in the right direction—the numbers are steadily improving each year. At present, they are at 52 percent white, and the city is at 36 percent white—the gap is closing. More importantly, people of all colors and nationalities are being saved, discipled, and worshiping together. God is surely smiling!

As a sidenote—when the present pastor was called to this church, he inherited a somewhat declining church with a general attitude of despair and discouragement, as well as a load of debt. Not anymore! Today they are debt-free, growing like crazy as a powerhouse for God. I wonder if their willingness to bring in *all* their community has something to do with their spiritual fitness.

Many churches might say, "Sure, we'll be glad to welcome anybody who wants to come—red, brown, yellow, black, and white. They are precious in His sight." That is good! That is as it should be. But there is a big difference in just being open to anyone who happens to show up and being intentional about bringing them in. The latter is far more commendable and is a reflection of the love of Christ! Other churches may say, "We don't have anyone living in our area other than our own race." Obviously, if they're not there, you can't bring them in. But keep your eyes open and pray that God will send them—there could be some around after all!

And perhaps there is another level of openheartedness to consider. Remember the church where we helped sponsor a funfest for the community? The tipping point was the suggestion to bring in a Hispanic staff person. It may have been tolerable for "those people" to come to "our" church, but the idea of giving one of them a leadership role turned the scenario into them *taking over* "our" church. The threat of control was the final straw. Quite a contrast to the church that intentionally places minorities in leadership roles!

Thank you for allowing me to share my heart with you. I pray that more and more of my brothers and sisters in Christ will find healing from the plague of prejudice as I did. Repentance and asking forgiveness of God are the required steps to set things right.

My prayer for our churches is that more and more will be convicted to reach out to races and nationalities outside our own. The initial step in the right direction is to pray and ask God to bring them to our doorstep then welcome them with open arms into our fellowship. Our church should not only look like our community, it should also look like the inhabitants of heaven.

Revelation 5:9 (NASB) describes a scene in the throne room of heaven, where people from "every tribe and tongue and people and nation" will be gathered together to worship the Lamb with a new song. What a glorious day that will be! Until then—we can have a foretaste of heaven in our churches as we worship together in all our ethnic diversity!

14

Are You Kidding Me?

You can't visit as many churches as I did and not have some unusual things happen. I've recorded here a collection of incidents that might be of interest—some are humorous, some are awkward or embarrassing, others are just out of the ordinary. Some will bring a laugh; others might make you roll your eyes or likely scratch your head and exclaim, "Are you kidding me?"

1. A common characteristic of every church of every size and every brand everywhere is that they *all* desperately need preschool workers and are constantly on a never-ending recruiting campaign!
2. Church sound systems either have a mind of their own, or they are cursed. Whatever the case may be, they seem to be a challenge in many, many churches, no matter the denomination.
3. About 95 percent of all churches use some form of the word *connect* in their promotion efforts and printed materials. It is often used in reference to their small groups, education ministry, or guest services. *Connection center, connection classes, get connected, connect with God, connect with others* seem to be popular usages of the term.
4. Many pastors promote and push the offering from the pulpit, sometimes sounding a bit too desperate!

5. It is hard for me to understand how so many churches can make such bad-tasting coffee—do they have workshops to train for this?

6. I received a welcome letter as a follow-up to a church visit. The envelope was addressed to "Mr. Bunny Griffin," and the greeting read, "Dear Bunny." Of course, I hopped on this with much eagerness!

7. Before the Lord's Supper was served, a minister announced to the attendees, "You have your choice of wine or grape juice, regular wheat bread or gluten-free bread." How accommodating!

8. I arrived at a church with the intention to attend their worship service and also a Bible study class. I had incorrect information about starting times, so I arrived in the middle of everything. I was too late for Bible study classes and too early for worship. I walked in the front door and found no one in sight. I weakly spoke a hello, and silence was my answer.

Then I heard footsteps in the distance and saw a man in a big hurry heading toward me. I said, "Excuse me, I am a visitor and—" Without slowing his pace a bit, he said, "You came at the wrong time." I quickly asked, "Is it time for worship?" He never slowed down a step and bluntly informed me that there were only classes going on, and worship started in about thirty-five minutes.

As he continued to briskly walk away from me, I asked, "Is there a class I can go to?" He responded, "Second door on your left," as he turned the corner, and the sound of the click of his heels on the stone floor faded. I proceeded to the second door on my left, gently and quietly turned the doorknob, and opened the door. As I was entering the classroom, the teacher said, "This class is full."

I quickly and silently retraced my steps, exited, softly closed the door, and went to their worship center and read my Bible while I waited for the service to begin. If I had been a legitimate visitor in search of God or looking for a church to join, it is highly likely I would have gone directly to my car and never returned—even at the correct time.

9. Arriving thirty minutes early at any church provides a great opportunity to meet and greet folks and also sample their coffee. I got my cup and looked for a place to sit. There was a seat available at a small table for two. To the man already seated there, I inquired, "May I join you?" He was pleasant and friendly. During our table talk, he learned that I was a visitor. Later, as we continued to converse, he said, "Listen, if you are looking for a church to join, this is it. We are the eating-est and partying-est church you will ever find!" Woo-hoo! I've found my niche!

10. As I sat in the large church worship center waiting for the service to start, I noticed the bulletin was exceptionally large. It was made up of fourteen pages, printed in Spanish and English, and the last four pages featured ads printed in color. A paragraph explained how to buy an "ad for the bulletin." The forty-four ads were for hair care, automotive shops, cafés, catering companies, ice-cream shops, funeral homes, day cares, life insurance, lawyers, yard work, knee surgery, eye care, remodeling, all types of contractors, house-cleaning, A/C and plumbing, dentists, and laundry service. I figured if you were bored during the service, you could read the ads. I was, and I did!

11. Just before the time in the service for the offering to be collected, the pastor encouraged everyone to pick up an envelope, and I did as instructed. As he continued speaking, I noticed the envelope had a familiar look with a place to fill in typical information. But there was one thing I had never seen before on an offering envelope. In the bottom left corner, it read, "Change due back: $_____." After asking a few questions later on, my assumption was proven to

be correct. A person could place a $10 bill in the envelope and indicate they wanted $5 back, and it would be returned in due time.

12. I was visiting a large church and really enjoying the service. The time came to welcome the visitors, and the pastor asked all guests to stand. I stood, along with about ten other visitors, while a member of the guest team gave each of us a card and a pen to fill it out. I sat down to fill it in, but the pastor asked me to remain standing and continue filling in the info. I finally finished and was instructed to remove the little red ribbon from the card and stick it on my shirt. This was no new routine to me, and I was certainly willing to cooperate, except my little visitor tag would not stick to my shirt. I pressed it to my shirt, but it would fall off immediately. This happened several times until my guest team member said to me, "I will get some Scotch tape." Before I could react, she was gone and back again. She placed the tag on my shirt and attached tape on all four sides of the ribbon. For sure, it stayed on!

13. Many churches give guests some kind of gift, most often distributed at the visitor desk or meet-the-pastor room. After 115 church visits, I have an abundance of gifts that include ballpoint pens, church brochures, tote bags, devotional books, pencils, bookmarkers, tracts, refrigerator magnets, calendars, eyeglass wipes, pencil holders, coffee cups, insulated coffee mugs, fingernail files, offering envelopes, small bottles of hand sanitizers and lotions, breath mints, packages of M&Ms, New Testaments, Hershey's candy kisses, pictures of Jesus, CDs of music and sermons, read-through-the-Bible charts, "get a free cup of coffee" tickets, six-inch rulers, key chains, rubber bracelets, WWJD pens, newsletters, small magnifying glass, church business cards, meal tickets to the church Wednesday night meal, $5 gift cards to Starbucks and Sonic, letter openers, koozies, note-

pads, small pocket cross, plastic scissors, highlighters, Bible verse cards, luggage tags, coasters, sticky tags, hand towels, rain hoods, measuring tapes, purse-size flashlights, etc.

Of course, a high percentage of these items have the church name and/or other information about the church printed on them. I am thinking about having a garage sale!

14. On one church visit, I was recognized by a sweet, grand-motherly type older lady as "the guy who plays the banjo." There I was—busted again! After a few moments of friendly conversation, she asked, "What are you doing way out here?" I began to tell her a little about my project and the book I might be writing. She immediately became quite animated and began to passionately tell me how I must put a chapter in my book about the "music in churches."

    Uh-oh, I knew what was coming—I had been there before. I mentally began to formulate an escape plan while she launched into her tirade. She was quite irate! With a good bit of emotion, she finally asked, "Do you know what the real problem is?" Before I could answer, she lowered her voice a bit and emphatically stated, "It's those damn drums!" There was a pause. I must say, she left me speechless!

15. As the pastor was conducting a baptismal service, an eight-year-old girl was the next candidate. She entered the baptistery and waved at her family, proudly sitting on the front row. The pastor introduced the girl and asked, "Have you asked Jesus into your heart to be your Lord and Savior?" She replied, "Don't you remember, you were there!" Duh!

16. The church was in the middle of a great time of praise and worship, with the words of the songs projected on the large screens in front of the auditorium. One verse of a certain song was followed by a segment of lyrics that repeated the word *oh* twenty-four times—you know that one, don't you? The word *oh* was printed on the screen twenty-four times— "Oh, oh, oh, oh, oh, oh, oh, oh, oh, oh, oh, oh, oh, oh, oh, oh,

oh, oh, oh, oh, oh, oh, oh, and oh." I was so focused on which *oh* to sing that I almost forgot the words! Oh no, oh no!

17. Before visiting a church, I always plotted my driving route. I would try to go to an early service at one church and then drive to another for a later service. While meeting with an early Sunday school group, I found myself trapped in the most boring class that surely ever existed on the face of the earth! To drive to my next church, I needed to leave a bit early. The problem was that I was sitting in the back of the room, and the main door was in the front of the room, right behind the teacher.

To leave, I would have to walk right by him and be seen by every person present. There was another door conveniently located in the back of the room only about fifteen feet from me. However, it had a sign on it that read, "EMERGENCY EXIT ONLY." Hmmmm, this was an emergency, wasn't it? Temptation overcame me. I quickly made my decision—I would slip out this door. I quietly eased out of my chair and tiptoed to the door. I opened it slowly and gently. Instantly a huge, ear-piercing siren went off! Yikes! Like any red-blooded coward would do, I ran like crazy to my car and never looked back! I am absolutely confident that my exit was the most exciting thing that happened in that place all day!

18. I could not believe I sat in another Bible study class where the teacher read the entire lesson from a quarterly. I mean, the entire lesson was read, word for word, including the discussion questions. I did have a bit of a problem hearing him because the snoring of folks around me sometimes drowned out the sound of his voice!

19. I loved watching the deacons and elders march into the church, all in step, while singing "Victory in Jesus." All were wearing black suits, white shirts, red ties, and white gloves. They entered at the front of the church, walked in forma-

tion in front of the pulpit, and continued to the front two pews. When the singing ended, the pastor entered and sat down in his podium chair. When he sat down, so did the other men. Cool!

20. The pastor asked all the guests to stand, and I did. He gave a warm welcome, invited us to fill out a visitor card, and told us an usher would give us a card and gift bag. I was handed my card and gift bag. I noticed immediately that the bag felt like it had nothing in it. When the service was over, I was warmly greeted and exited for my car. When I was inside my car, I looked into the gift bag and discovered it contained one short golf pencil, two offering envelopes, a church business card, and one peppermint candy! It's the thought that counts, right?

21. It was a cold November morning, and the constant drizzle made it even more uncomfortable. I had about a thirty-minute drive to a church on the north side of Houston. I really wanted a cup of hot coffee, and I was hoping this church had a good supply. I planned to attend both a Bible study class and then the worship service. When I made it to a classroom, I was greeted with the wonderful aroma of coffee brewing. Ahhh! There was a large pot of hot coffee, and I was sure my name was on it. I was hoping to find a doughnut to go with it, but I was out of luck. I got my cup of hot coffee and took a seat.

After just a couple of sips, a lady carrying two Shipley's bags entered and announced, "Sorry, I'm late. Besides bad weather, the traffic was terrible! I've got doughnuts and kolaches. Come get 'em while they're hot!" Without hesitating, I got up, placed my cup of black coffee in the chair, and headed toward the doughnut table. As I gratefully grabbed a kolache and a doughnut, a friendly gentleman began a conversation with me. I was appreciative of his welcoming gesture, and as we talked, I glanced toward my chair where I had left my cup of coffee. I noticed another cup of coffee sitting on the chair next to mine. I think someone was doing the same thing I was.

As the conversation was about to end, I glanced at my chair just in time to see a man come over, pick up *my* cup of coffee and begin to indulge. His first swallow brought a frown to his face—then he headed to the sugar and cream. When I reached my chair and picked up *his* cup of coffee, my suspicions were confirmed—it was light tan in color. Seeing him loading my cup with sugar and cream, I inconspicuously placed his cup in a nearby trash can. I passed my coffee-snatching friend as I returned to the coffeepot for a fresh cup. As he stirred the contents of my cup really well, I couldn't help but question, "How's the coffee?"

22. In visiting such a large number of churches, I was introduced to numerous types of bulletins. On one particular church visit, I noticed something listed under the order of service that I had never seen or heard of before. First on the program was the prelude followed by the Sunday school report—I was familiar with both of those. I was looking forward to the third item on the program because it was new to me. It was called simply the chant. As I waited for the service to begin, I noticed that only a few elderly people were sitting in the very large choir loft. The left side of the platform was set up for the praise band. One musician was in position at the electronic organ ready for the prelude. The drums, bass, guitar, and several horns were visible on stage, but no other musicians were to be seen.

The service began at the appointed time. After the Sunday school report concluded, the organist began to play, and the people began to sing. As the singing started, the choir members, musicians, and white-gloved ushers began to take their places. The music grew in intensity. The excitement expanded and hit a crescendo when the pastor and his staff walked down the center aisle and took their places on the stage. It was a wonderful experience, and I enjoyed every note, verse, and chorus of the chant.

23. In being greeted as a newcomer, people typically would ask questions such as, "Do you live close by?" "Are you a member of another church?" "Do you think you would like to come back?" Inevitably I would be asked, "Where do you work?" or "What do you do?" Not wanting to reveal I was a retired pastor on a secret-church-shopper mission, I simply responded by saying, "I'm retired," and hoped it would end at that. I certainly did not want to lie to anyone for the sake of maintaining anonymity, but I also did not want to blow my cover.

After a bit of thought in my self-preservation mind-set, I came up with an answer that I considered truthful but admittedly a trifle misleading. When they asked, "What did you do before you retired?" I simply answered, "I was in human resources." No one ever questioned me further after that reply—thank you, Jesus!

Hope you got a grin reading this stuff! If you didn't, you might want to check your pulse.

15

That's a Wrap!

If you have ever been in a recording studio, it is always a relief to hear the producer say, "That's a wrap!" This refers to the end of a recording session. A wrap means it is over, finished, done, *fini*, *no mas!*

I have written many musical arrangements for banjo solos and for banjo bands. Always, after the wrap, in my head, I have a syncopated rhythm pattern, lingering bass line, a certain drumbeat, or harmony part I wish I had incorporated into the score. There is always something else I could have added! I learned a long time ago that when it comes to recording a CD or writing a musical arrangement, I am not ever really through—I just have to quit and say, "That's a wrap."

The same scenario can be applied to this book. When I placed the last period behind the last word of the last sentence in the previous chapter, it was a wrap in theory only. Other thoughts, impressions, and ideas are still in my heart and head—here are a few.

Personal Life Lessons—How God Changed Me

God is much bigger than I ever imagined. Throughout my secret-church-shopper experience, I was continually amazed to see God at work in unexpected places—the scope of His reach is far and wide.

I was *not* as important in His kingdom as I thought I was. What a humbling experience! I'm considering writing another book titled *All the Things I Learned After I Thought I Knew It All.*

I had some opinions about other denominations that were just plain wrong. Having unintentionally acquired some negative attitudes, it was refreshing to get out of my own denominational box and discover the truth for myself.

Having this church-visiting experience years ago would have made me a more usable servant of the Lord as well as a more effective pastor. This is a primary motivation for sharing my experience with others unable to do what I did.

The Final Takeaways

I am encouraged that many churches are doing an excellent job in advancing the kingdom of God. No matter the size of the congregation or the style of the service, what counts is whether Christ is elevated to His proper place and the gospel of salvation by grace is preached.

Denominations can be a huge dividing force within the family of God. Those who share the same basic tenets of the faith should focus on that commonality to transcend differences regarding minor issues. The body of Christ united together across denominational lines could more effectively reach the world with the message of salvation.

Many pastors and churches seem to be more in love with their traditions of worship than with God Himself. When the form and ceremonies of religion are routinely practiced without the emphasis on the Savior, worship becomes empty, hollow, and meaningless. God wants our hearts in a personal relationship with Him.

Churches need to know how to deal with spiritually dead people. Many regular churchgoers have never received eternal life through faith in Jesus Christ. They need to hear the preaching of the powerful, life-giving Word of God, the Bible. A church must focus on providing the biblical message of salvation by grace through faith in Jesus Christ, or all else is in vain. Eternal salvation is the main thing—let's let the main thing be the main thing!

My main goal has been *to provide firsthand information for the church to advance the kingdom of God.* That is what this book is all about, and I pray the goal will be accomplished.

I have strongly felt from my first church visit to the last word written in this book that the entire project has been a *God thing.* All praise, glory, honor, and credit belongs to our Lord!

Thank you for sharing this incredible journey with me! Now I'm done—*that's a wrap!*

Give 'em *heaven!*

Buddy Griffin

APPENDIX

BUDDY GRIFFIN'S STATEMENT OF BELIEF

As I have prepared *What in Heaven Is Going On at Church?* I evaluated and graded all types of churches. The obvious question is what criteria and from what perspective did I make my observations and come to my conclusions. The Bible, my spiritual stance, my convictions are the filters that all information passed through, which led to my results. Therefore, anyone interested in this information must know *where I stand* spiritually, which was the primary influence in all my research and conclusions.

I believe…

In the reality of one true God, eternal and infinite, existing as three persons—Father, Son, and Holy Spirit. Man was made in the image of God. The fall of man from God's grace by sin put man in the position of needing forgiveness in order that his fellowship with God might be restored. God sent His son, Jesus Christ, into the world to take man's sin upon Himself. Jesus was begotten by the Holy Spirit, born of the Virgin Mary, and is fully God and fully man, the only sinless person who ever lived. As the Lamb of God, He took man's sin upon Himself as He died on the cross, thus satisfying God's holy demands for all mankind. He was buried and was resurrected on the third day following His crucifixion.

After appearing to various people during a period of forty days, He ascended into heaven and is the only mediator between God and man. All who personally receive Him through faith obtain forgiveness of sin on the basis of His shed blood and are declared righteous on the basis of His personally sinless life. When a person confesses the fact that he is a sinner and acknowledges Jesus Christ as his Lord and Savior, his spirit is reborn. He becomes a new creation, a child of God, a member of the true *church*, is indwelt by the Holy Spirit, and is guaranteed eternity in heaven with God.

This salvation is not the result of any human effort but is the free gift of God's grace in Jesus Christ. Jesus destroyed all the works of Satan—who, as god of this world, is allowed to continue for now to blind the eyes of those who do not believe. Satan leads a host of fallen beings who are his aides in warring against believers. Believers must be aware of the reality of spiritual warfare and know that victory is theirs through the application of scriptural truth and the presence and power of the indwelling Holy Spirit.

God sent His Holy Spirit with gifts to the church to empower believers for witnessing of Jesus, as well as to be comforter and teacher, until Jesus comes again. The Holy Spirit witnesses not unto Himself but to the risen Christ. He regenerates, seals, anoints, and sets apart the believer to a holy life. Christ ordained the observance of water baptism and the Lord's Supper until He returns. The Bible was written by men who wrote under the direct control, inspiration, and anointing of the Holy Spirit of God.

The Bible does not contain the Word of God; it is the Word of God—infallible, inerrant, the only written revelation that God has given to man. It increases man's faith as well as instructs and corrects him that he might become holy, separated from the world, and set apart unto God. The main theme of the Bible is God's plan of salvation in Jesus Christ. Everything in the life of every human being is directly or indirectly affected by his attitude about the Bible—whether or not he accepts it as the inspired Word of God. It is the supreme and final authority in all matters about which it speaks.

FOR MEN ONLY!

Thank you for picking up my book. I sincerely appreciate it and am honored and humbled.

From the beginning of my 16-month, 115-church-visiting trek as a secret church shopper, I have had one main goal that has been my driving force: to provide firsthand information for the church to advance the kingdom of God.

During this process, several people have asked me why I did it. My reasons are explained in chapter 1. However, there is another huge influencing force behind my actions, which I will share only with you men. When folks yield to our Lord, snuggle up to Him, and allow Him to lead, guide, and direct our lives, the abundant life that emerges is just so wonderful, fulfilling, and satisfying that I want everyone to experience it.

One occurrence in my life that changed everything involved the relationship between my father and me. I experienced one of those unbelievable happenings. It concerns the "father wound" I had carried all my life, how I was delivered, and the reconciliation with my father that occurred after sixty years.

I know there are some men reading this who also carry the father wound. You may have never even heard the term, but you are at odds with your dad; and besides hurting you, it affects your lifestyle. Unresolved conflict, distrust, ill will, anger, resentment, and fear are all by-products of an unresolved father wound. The misery and stress this brings to a man's life are horrific. My prayer is that by reading my testimony, it will help a man begin to deal with his father wound and lead to actions that bring reconciliation and healing with his father.

The following is my story—may it bless you!

At a family retreat I was leading in the Texas hill country on March 12, 2005, my friend, David Chapek, told me with great enthusiasm about a men's meeting he was attending called the Quest for Authentic Manhood. I saw an unusual amount of excitement in the eyes of this NASA engineer, and that intrigued me.

David invited me to attend one of the Quest meetings, which was being held at University Baptist Church in the NASA area near Houston, Texas. He also mentioned that Quest was part of a ministry called Men's Fraternity and that the author, Dr. Robert Lewis, would be speaking at an upcoming breakfast meeting. David invited me to attend. I was interested, and I eagerly made plans to be there. I really wanted to learn more about Men's Fraternity.

On Tuesday, March 15, at 7:00 a.m., I drove to the University Baptist Church to attend the session; and I, along with eighty other men, enjoyed a hearty breakfast. Dr. Lewis conducted an instructional workshop afterward. His presentation was titled "What Men Need and How the Church Can Help."

During his presentation, he spoke about his relationship with his dad and how difficult it had been and how it had affected his life. I really related to what he was saying. The more he talked, the more I realized we had a lot in common when it came to how we were raised and our individual relationships with our dads. Dr. Lewis's presentation included an old photo of him, his two brothers, and his dad. The photo was taken when Dr. Lewis was in his late teens.

If you looked real hard, you could make out the dark, shadowy silhouette of his dad, standing in the background behind his three sons in the dense shade of the tree. His dad was wearing a white dress shirt with his sleeves rolled up to his elbows. His face was hidden by gray shadows, and you could barely make out his presence. Dr. Lewis used this photo to illustrate the fact that his dad was in the "picture of his life" but always in the background and out of reach and out of touch with his sons.

Ouch! That hit home with me. My own father's presence and influence in my life could be characterized using the same photo. My father never told me he loved me. He never hugged me, and I could never please him or measure up to his expectations. As I was listening, I felt like someone punched me in the stomach because what Dr. Lewis was sharing was exactly like my relationship with my dad, and I just didn't want to go there.

During the coffee break, I walked over to get a bottle of water, and the only other person at the table was Dr. Lewis. I introduced myself, and we exchanged greetings. Our conversation went like this:

"Dr. Lewis, what you said about your dad really disturbed and hurt me."

"You must have had the same type of situation, Buddy."

"Yes, I did."

"Is your dad still alive?"

"Yes, he is ninety-four and lives in a retirement center."

"Buddy, what are you going to do about it?"

I was a bit confused and responded, "Do about what?"

"About your relationship with your dad. I know there is a lot of hurt and pain in your life because of your poor relationship with your dad. What are you going to do about it?"

His statement and question really shocked me. I had never been asked anything like that in my entire life and really did not know how to respond. Then Dr. Lewis said something to me that nearly buckled my knees: "Someday you will stand at his casket. Will you be filled with anger and unresolved hate toward him, or will you have peace and love toward him? It is a choice every man must make."

"Well, Dr. Lewis, I will pray about it."

"That's fine, Buddy, but that is a 'church answer'—real men *do* something about it."

"What should I do?"

"You need to go to your dad and say that you need him to tell you that he loves you and you need him to hug you. You have a deep father wound, and you need to take care of it. Going to your dad and confronting him is a great way to start the healing process."

The coffee break was over. I thanked Dr. Lewis. We shook hands, and we headed back to the auditorium for the conclusion of his presentation. From that moment on, I didn't hear much of what Dr. Lewis said. I could not help but think about doing what he suggested, about confronting my dad face-to-face. I found myself scared, a bit dizzy, nauseated, confused, doubtful, and trying to conceal a hurt heart, and I experienced some other emotions I cannot even describe.

Exactly a week later, on Tuesday, March 22, a dear friend of mine, Jim Laucher, was in my office waiting for an upcoming two-hour counseling session that was to begin at 10:00 a.m. Neither one of us were looking forward to the session. Jim is a professional counselor, and he was there to be a witness to the meeting. About 9:50 a.m., the counselee called and cancelled the meeting. The cancellation allowed me two hours of free time. I told Jim what had happened at the Quest meeting and asked him if he would go with me to visit my dad so he could pray for me as I spoke to my dad and provide moral support. He, being a caring Christian counselor and dear friend, said, "Let's go."

Driving over to University Place retirement center was scary for me. On the one hand, I anxiously wanted to visit with my dad;

and on the other hand, I was gripped by fear and dread. I wanted to turn around several times and head back to the church, but with Jim's encouragement and our Lord's strength, somehow I made it to University Place. I parked, and Jim and I made our way to dad's apartment, number 225.

After a brief, how-are-you visit, I said to him, "Dad, I need to tell you something you might not understand…I really need you to tell me you love me." I could tell my statement shocked him, and he hesitantly and meekly responded, "I love everybody."

I said, "No, Dad, no…I want you to tell *me!*"

He hesitated and finally said in a low tone, "I love you."

I quickly responded, "Dad, I want you to say it in a loud voice so I can hear it really good."

I could tell this was difficult for him, but he finally did speak in a very quiet voice. Then I said, "Dad, I need for you to hug me!" He gave me a brief, sideways hug with one arm. I responded, "Dad, I need a real hug…put your arms around me and hug me."

He immediately said, "I have to go." But where?

As he was leaving his apartment, I told him that every time I came to see him in the future, I wanted us to do the same thing. I could tell it was more than difficult for him. I knew it was a strange occurrence in both of our lives, and I felt a twinge of being sorry for him. He walked out of the room, and Jim and I left. Jim was praising our Lord and slapping me on the back and giving me "atta-boys." I felt such relief!

I went to see my dad at least once a week and sometimes more than that. It became obvious and exciting to me that, with every visit, our talks and interaction got better and better. On my eighth visit, a miracle occurred. I walked into his apartment, and he said, "Come here, son." I did, and he began to hug me and boldly tell me that he loved me. My tears were evidence that the dam of loneliness, resentment, and fear had broken within me.

My dad's tears and smiles indicated the new joy and relationship he had discovered. My weekly visits got to the point that the "I love yous" and hugs were commonplace, and we both looked forward to them. Finally, after all these years, my ninety-four-year-old dad and I, his sixty-four-year-old son, had a neat father-son relationship— just like it should be! Praise God!

We eventually had to move Dad from independent living to an assisted-living unit. Again, I kept up my regular visits with him. They were all good, loving, and kind, and I really looked forward to meeting with him. His hearing and eyesight were quickly diminishing, and his mental state was also suffering. On August 13, I received a call from a staff member informing me that they were transferring my dad to Memorial Hermann Hospital because there had been some serious changes in his physical condition, and he was critically ill.

I left work and drove to the ER. Dad was already there in the ICU. I visited with the doctors, and they informed me that my dad had double pneumonia, and it was so advanced that they really could not do much for him, especially considering his age and deteriorating health condition. A few days later, he was placed in hospice care. My weekly visits now turned into daily visits.

On August 28, 2007, my wife, Sandy, and I visited him around 9:00 p.m. It was like all the other visits. He was just lying in the bed, on his back, with his eyes closed. He had not spoken a word or shown any signs of improvement since he was admitted to the hospital fifteen days earlier. Like our other visits, we would meet with the hospice staff and then go see Dad for just a few minutes. I walked over to his bed, rubbed his hand, kissed him on his forehead, and said, "I love you, Dad."

It was time for us to go, and as I reached for the doorknob to leave, my dad said in a loud, strong, and clear voice, "I love you, Buddy." I was stunned! I am so glad Sandy was there to hear what he said, or I would have thought I just imagined it. As we left his room and were walking to our car, I told Sandy, "My dad is going to die tomorrow. I just know it."

The next day, August 29, Sandy received a call from the hospice nurse at about 10:00 a.m., informing us that there had been "significant changes" in my dad's condition, and we should come to the hospital. Sandy called me, and I left the office immediately. She was closer and arrived at Dad's room before I did. The hospice staff informed us that it was just a "matter of time." I sat by his bed and held his hand. How grateful to our Lord and relieved I was that my dad and I had healed our father-son relationship. It was obvious that his time was short, and he was about to graduate to heaven. I was holding his hand when he took his last breath at 3:07 p.m. He was ninety-six years-old. I proudly conducted his memorial service.

In September of 2008, I was the presenter for the Quest for Authentic Manhood at Sagemont Church. Over the weeks to come, many of the five hundred men in attendance discovered their own father wound and dealt with it in a godly and healing way. I not only had the head knowledge about the father wound, but I had the heart knowledge too.

Thank you, Lord, Dr. Robert Lewis, David Chapek, Jim Laucher, and Men's Fraternity.

To God be the glory!

ABOUT THE AUTHOR

In 1951, during a Billy Graham Crusade held at Rice University football stadium, a ten-year-old Buddy Griffin gave his life to Christ. Seven years later, the Lord called, and he committed his life to full-time Christian ministry. In January of 2014, he retired after fifty years in the ministry. The last twelve years, he served as pastor of men and prayer at Sagemont Church in Houston, Texas.

Buddy has served in churches of all sizes, ranging from start-up to mega in a variety of ministry roles. He has been a featured speaker, conference leader, and seminar presenter locally, statewide, and on the national level. In 2007, the National Council of Men's Ministries presented him with the Pastor of the Year award.

With a heart for missions, Buddy has led recent mission trips to Kenya, Tanzania, and Mexico and participated in others through the years to various European nations, Japan, and Hong Kong.

Buddy is also an entertainer and has spread the happy sounds of the banjo and ukulele across the USA and abroad. In 2005, he was inducted into the Banjo Hall of Fame. He is the founder and director of the seventy-member All Stars Youth Banjo Band. Buddy is also an avid bass fisherman. He reasons, "Since God made the world three-fourths water, shouldn't a man spend three-fourths of his time fishing?"

Buddy and his wife, Sandy, live in Houston, Texas, and enjoy two grown children, their spouses, and two supercool grandkids.

Buddy & Sandy Griffin
50th Wedding Anniversary Photo

Contact information:
Buddy Griffin
2007 Mardel Court
Houston, Texas 77077

The
Red Beast

of related interest

Anger Management Games for Children
Deborah M. Plummer
Illustrated by Jane Serrurier
ISBN 978 1 84310 628 9

Why do I have to?
A Book for Children Who Find Themselves Frustrated by Everyday Rules
Laurie Leventhal-Belfer
Illustrated by Luisa Montaini-Klovdahl
ISBN 978 1 84310 891 7

Caring for Myself
A Social Skills Storybook
Christy Gast and Jane Krug
Photographs by Kotoe Laackman
ISBN 978 1 84310 872 6 (Hardback)
ISBN 978 1 84310 887 0 (Paperback)

Autistic Planet
Jennifer Elder
Illustrated by Marc Thomas and Jennifer Elder
ISBN 978 1 84310 842 9